SpringerBriefs in Education

Open and Distance Education

Series editors

Insung Jung, International Christian University, Mitaka-shi, Tokyo, Japan
Colin Latchem, Perth, Western Autralia, Australia

More information about this series at http://www.springer.com/series/15238

Adnan Qayyum · Olaf Zawacki-Richter
Editors

Open and Distance Education in Australia, Europe and the Americas

National Perspectives in a Digital Age

 Springer Open

Editors
Adnan Qayyum
Pennsylvania State University
State College, PA
USA

Olaf Zawacki-Richter
University of Oldenburg
Oldenburg, Niedersachsen
Germany

ISSN 2211-1921   ISSN 2211-193X   (electronic)
SpringerBriefs in Education
ISSN 2509-4335   ISSN 2509-4343   (electronic)
SpringerBriefs in Open and Distance Education
ISBN 978-981-13-0297-8   ISBN 978-981-13-0298-5   (eBook)
https://doi.org/10.1007/978-981-13-0298-5

Library of Congress Control Number: 2018939993

Printed on acid-free paper

This Springer imprint is published by the registered company Springer Nature Singapore Pte Ltd.
part of Springer Nature
The registered company address is: 152 Beach Road, #21-01/04 Gateway East, Singapore 189721,
Singapore

Contents

Open and Distance Education in a Digital Age

Adnan Qayyum and Olaf Zawacki-Richter

Introduction

Open and distance education is changing. Distance education (DE) in higher education is changing in size, location and shape. Generally speaking, the size of distance education is growing in many parts of the world as more people are enrolled in DE offerings. In Brazil, there was an enrolment growth of 900% from 2000 to 2010 (de Oliveira Neto and dos Santos 2010). In Russia and Turkey, nearly 50% of all higher education students enrolled in open or distance education programs (Zawacki-Richter et al. 2015). The number of people enrolled in DE courses and offerings may have never been higher in many countries.

The size of DE is growing on the supply side as well as the demand side. On the supply side, more DE is being offered by institutions that have conventionally offered DE and by new entrants. Historically, distance education was the mandate of single mode institutions that specialized in distance learning provisions, or dual mode universities that provide on-campus programs and offered DE from a continuing education department. Dual mode institutions that offered DE were universities and colleges that made "access" an important principle in their university mission. Their distance education departments were usually tucked away in continuing education, extension or adult education departments. The single mode universities were either distance teaching universities, like the University of South Africa or the FernUniversität in Germany, or open universities like the Open University in the United Kingdom or the Korean National Open University. From their start in the 1960s and 70s open

A. Qayyum (✉)
Pennsylvania State University, State College, PA, USA
e-mail: adnan@psu.edu

O. Zawacki-Richter
Carl von Ossietzky Universität Oldenburg, Oldenburg, Germany
e-mail: olaf.zawacki.richter@uni-oldenburg.de

© The Author(s) 2018
A. Qayyum and O. Zawacki-Richter (eds.), *Open and Distance Education in Australia, Europe and the Americas*, SpringerBriefs in Open and Distance Education, https://doi.org/10.1007/978-981-13-0298-5_1

1

universities represented a novel educational organization. They increased access to higher education by opening the admissions requirements for entering universities. This was combined with the flexible delivery of distance education. Single mode open universities have continued to grow over the decades. They constitute most of the world's largest "mega-universities" (Daniels 1996, p. 8), universities which enrol over 100,000 students. The demand for open and distance learning opportunities especially in developing countries is enormous. Hence, new open universities have been established in more recent times like the Open University of Nigeria (in 2002), the Arab Open University (in 2002), the Cyprus Open University (in 2004), and the Wawasan Open University in Malaysia (in 2006). The Open University of Nigeria has grown exponentially, serving over 200,000 students today.

The size and location of DE is changing as an increasing number and type of institutions are offering DE programs and courses. Within many conventional open and distance education institutions, the number of DE offerings has increased, as supply follows demand. But now more residential universities, as a whole, are offering DE courses and programs. Historically, dual mode universities usually excluded institutions that prided themselves on their exclusiveness. Elite universities like Tshingua or Stanford were elite partly by their admissions and price barriers. They had marginal, if any, interest in the access mission of DE. Now dual mode institutions that prided themselves on their exclusiveness are increasingly offering online courses. In Europe, over 80% of higher education institutions are offering online courses, where the course is delivered primarily to geographically distant students (Gaebel et al. 2014, p. 7). In countries like Brazil, Malaysia and the United States the growing demand for DE has seen a growth in private sector DE providers. The number and type of DE institutions continues to grow. DE is offered from more institutions in more locations than ever before.

The shape of DE is changing. A common format for a DE offering is a course delivered by a university. But it is certainly not the only format. DE has always been offered in more formats than conventional education. Fundamentally, DE has been education that uses information and communication technologies (ICTs) to overcome the separation between learners and educators. Freed from the need to be in the same location at the same time, usually a classroom, DE offerings have ranged from self-paced independent study, where students learn mainly on their own, to cohort-based collaborative courses. These are delivered either asynchronously or synchronously depending on learning goals and technologies available. Historically, DE providers have used successive generations of ICTs from print correspondence and postal delivery to radio broadcasts, television, videoconferencing, computer conferencing and the internet. New formats for DE offerings have continuously emerged using new technologies and novel design. Massive open online courses (MOOCs) are the most high-profile recent example of a novel format. Large open access courses are certainly not new in DE history, nor is providing educational offerings that have the option of accreditation or not. Large scale open educational programs have been offered for decades like the national radio farm forums in Canada in the 1940s, the language education radio broadcasts offered in Kenya and Lesotho in the 1980s (Perraton 2006), *Funkkolleg* educational broadcasts for certificates in West Germany, formal educational courses via television broadcasts by the Central China and Radio and Television University, and the nonformal education programs of British Broadcasting Corporation telecasts. Since the advent of the internet and mobile technologies there seems to be an acceleration of different formats. As the world is increasingly connected to the internet via various devices, online education in multiple formats has captured the interest of students and educational institutions. The increased use of "blended", "flipped", "massive", "distributed", "mobile", "flexible", and "nonformal" learning or education are often manifestations of different DE formats. The shape of DE continues to broaden.

The Purpose and Structure of This Book

Growth in education enrollments and use of digital ICTs in education do not show signs of slowing. In the short term these trends should continue to affect the size, shape and location of DE. Certainly, open and distance education is changing, and there has been much research on how digital ICTS are affecting DE teaching, learning, design and even management issues. But we do not know how these changes are affecting different countries. There is a lack of DE research on macro level issues about DE systems (Zawacki-Richter and Anderson 2014) including: the relationship of DE with higher education systems in various countries; the organization and structure of higher DE systems; how changes in DE are affecting open universities; what are major challenges that DE providers are encountering? This book is the first of two volumes aimed at describing how ODE is evolving to reflect the needs and circumstance of the national higher education systems in these various countries. A second goal is to compare how DE is organized and structured in various countries.

Methodology

Nations are the focus of these two volumes because educational systems are usually organized according to the nation state. In some places education policies and decisions are made mainly at the local state or provincial level, as we see for Germany and Canada discussed in this book. However, even in such settings, the overall national context is the starting premise of educational policy making (Baker 2009, p. 958). This makes nations an important unit of analysis and measurement for most international and comparative educational work.

Nearly all the nations chosen for these two volumes have a long tradition in DE and have seen substantial changes in the applications of ODE in recent years. Geographical and regional diversity were important in selecting countries. Some countries like Spain, Indonesia and Nigeria have strong DE traditions, but were not included as only 12 countries could be described and analyzed in these two books. Australia, Brazil, Canada, China, Germany, India, Russia, South Africa, South Korea,

Turkey, United Kingdom, United States have strong DE traditions. Choosing these countries also allowed for describing and comparing DE that affects over half the world's population.

The goal in this book is not just to describe what his happening in different countries but to compare what is happening. Comparison is not a straightforward process. Countries have different social, political and educational histories that must be acknowledged. Comparing requires a *tertium comparationis*, "a third comparison" or common points of reference, so that countries can be compared with common variables while accounting for different histories, resources and priorities of educational systems (Raivola 1985). The goal in the book is not only to let the reader discover similarities and differences. The goal is to distinguish different approaches and identify models of the relationships between DE and higher education systems.

To create common points of comparison, the authors of each country chapter were asked to address the following guiding questions about DE:

1. What is the function and position of distance education within the national higher education system?
2. Which are the major DE teaching and research institutions?
3. What is the history and past of distance education including online education?
4. What is the relationship between DE and more established and older campus-based, residential institutions?
5. What is the relationship between public and private sector online and distance education?
6. What are the regulatory frameworks for DE? What are important policies for online and distance education?
7. What are estimated student enrollments for online and distance education programs?
8. What are probably important future developments and issues for online and distance education?

Structure of the Books

The books are organized into two volumes. They are roughly organized by continents, though Russia and Turkey are in both Europe and Asia. The first volume covers Australia, Europe and the Americas and includes chapters from Australia, Brazil, Canada, Germany, the United Kingdom and the United States. The second book covers Asia, Africa and the Middle East and include China, India, Russia, South Africa, South Korea and Turkey. Each volume includes a concluding chapter comparing the countries described.

Experts in DE from each of the 12 countries were invited. All authors have deep experience as DE researchers, practitioners or journal editors of the countries about which they write. Each country is described and analysed from two perspectives. In the main chapter of each country, the authors address the guideline questions in their own format. There is no template structure, so authors can share their insights according to their own approaches. After the main chapter is a second section called the commentary. It is written by a different DE expert from that country. These are not critiques of the country chapter. They are commentaries about open and distance education in that country. They are short accounts on DE from the perspective another expert in the country to further validate the results.

In each of the books the countries are presented alphabetically. Chapter 2 in this book is about Australia. Colin Latchem describes how DE in Australia has gone through three historical phases: correspondence education/external studies from 1910 to 1970; distance education from 1970 to 1980s; and open, flexible and online learning from 1980s to the present. Online and flexible learning have changed the size and shape of DE in Australia. The number of students studying at a distance has increased in Australia, from just over 10% in the 1990s to 18% in 2013. At the same time nine percent of higher education students are enrolled in multi-modal learning, which includes blended learning, flipped learning and other approaches that allow for taking courses partially off campus. This growth, along with MOOCs and increased connections of formal and nonformal education, is creating something different from "distance education" as it is conventionally understood.

Frederic Litto states that DE offerings in Brazil are fairly recent in any sustained way, despite a few offerings via radio in the 1930s, television in the 1950s and correspondence in the 1990s. 1996 was the key year in the development of DE in Brazil when degrees via distance were given equal status as those earned via face-to-face education. From that time, the growth in distance education, particularly online education, came gradually and then suddenly. In 2002, 25 mainly public institutions were offering distance based higher education courses. By 2015, over 300 higher education institutions could offer DE courses and nearly 80% of them were private institution. There are now over one million undergraduate students alone enrolled in distance education based programs.

Tony Bates describes how Canada has moved very strongly into online education in the past 25 years. In fact, Canada has been an innovative leader in distance education, particularly online education. The first web-based learning management system, WebCT, was created at the University of British Columbia, and the first MOOC was offered at the University of Manitoba. The innovations have emerged predominantly from public institutions as there is very little private sector distance education provision in Canada. There are a couple of single mode public institutions—Athabasca University and Tele-Universite Quebec—and many dual mode public institutions offering online education. There is also no national government involvement in education and no national ministry or department of education. There are, however, several meta-organizations that help foster and coordinate online education.

Ulrich Bernath and Joachim Stöter discuss the changes that have occurred in DE in Germany. There is a long tradition of DE there dating back over 150 years. DE was especially important in the former East Germany where nearly 25% of all higher education degrees were granted via distance education. In West Germany radio based DE was popular in the 1960s and FernUniverstät—a single mode DE provider—was opened in 1975. But changes in DE in the 1990s were affected by the reunification of Germany and the growth in the use of ICTs in all higher education. Of Germany's 427 higher education institutions, only a small percentage offer DE programs. Still, enrollments in distance learning have continued to grow in more recent times, in both degree granting and non-degree granting programs.

Anne Gaskell reminds us that the late Nelson Mandela was a distance education student of a university in the United Kingdom. While in prison during apartheid South Africa, he studied law through the University of London's International Programmes, a distance and flexible learning program that has been operating for over 150 years. The UK has a long rich tradition in DE, including being the country to start the first Open University. The initiative gave rise to many other open universities throughout the world. More recently, ICT use has grown in higher education in the UK but the Open University continues to be the most important DE institution in the country. Changes in government funding policies are a concern for DE in the UK as is the growing use of MOOCs. In response to the latter, the Open University has created its own MOOC platform and partnership.

Michael Beaudoin provides a long view of DE in the United States. While most discussions in the U.S. are about online education, there is a long tradition of DE delivered by other media over many generations. The U.S. has over 6500 higher education institutions that includes a public, private non-profit, and private for-profit universities. DE has a long tradition mainly with public institutions. With the advent of online education, private non-profits and private for-profit institutions have become involved. Unlike many other countries, the U.S. has a mix of a state and market funded model for higher education. The cost of higher education is a major issue and this has affected DE enrollments. Online education has grown overall in the past decade, but this has mainly been at public and private non-profit institutions. Private for-profit online providers have seen enrollments drop in recent years.

Terminology

As DE has changed shapes, many new terms are used to define activities that are the same as, or overlap with, distance education. Common terms include online learning, e-learning, distance learning, open learning, blended learning and flexible learning (see for example Orr et al. 2017). The numerous terms can cause conceptual confusion. DE and online education overlap but not all distance education is online and not all online education is via distance. Some have argued that online education originates separately from distance education, with the former more focused on collaborative learning while the latter still has a focus on independent learning (Garrison 2009). This is not a book about only on online learning or e-learning, though they are discussed by authors when they overlap with distance education. Guri-Rosenblit (2005) argued that distance education in most higher education systems is not delivered through the new electronic media, and e-learning in most universities and colleges all over the world is not used for distance education purposes. In this book authors address whether this is the case. In many countries, online learning or e-learning are a small if growing aspect of DE. But even here, the fundamental experience of distance education still matters—the separation of the student from the instructor (Kanuka and Conrad 2003). While physical distance may matter less in some countries, it is still an important reality for people in many countries. Indeed, the authors identify that the terms distance education and open learning have a different meaning in, say Russia and Turkey, then they do in Brazil or the United Kingdom. As such, distance education, in all its varieties and platforms, is the focus of these two books.

References

Baker, D. P. (2009). The invisible hand of world education culture. In G. Sykes, B. Schneider, & D. N. Plank (Eds.), *Handbook of education policy research*. New York: Routledge.

Daniels, J. (1996). *Mega-universities and knowledge media*. London: Kogan Page.

de Oliveira Neto, J. D., & dos Santos, E. M. (2010). Analysis of the methods and research topics in a sample of the Brazilian distance education publications, 1992 to 2007. *American Journal of Distance Education, 24*(3), 119–134. https://doi.org/10.1080/08923647.2010.497325.

Gaebel, M., Kupriyanova, V., Morais, R., & Colucci, E. (2014). *E-learning in European higher education institutions*. Belgium: European University Association.

Garrison, R. (2009). Implications of online learning for the conceptual development and practice of distance education. *Journal of Distance Education, 23*(2), 93–104.

Guri-Rosenblit, S. (2005). Distance education and e-learning: Not the Same thing. *Higher Education, 49*(4)467–493.

Kanuka, H., & Conrad, D. (2003). The name of the game: Why "Distance Education" says it all. *Quarterly Review of Distance Education, 4*(4), 385–393.

Orr, D., Weller, M., & Farrow, R. (2017). *Models for online, open, flexible and technology enhanced higher education—Results of a global analysis*. Presentation at the World Conference on Online Learning. Toronto: International Council for Open and Distance Education.

Perraton, H. (2006). *Open and distance learning in the developing world* (2nd ed.). London: Routledge.

Raivola, R. (1985). What is comparison? Methodological and philosophical considerations. *Comparative Education Review, 29*(3), 362–374.

Zawacki-Richter, O., & Anderson, T. (Eds.). (2014). *Online distance education—Towards a research agenda*. Athabasca, Edmonton, Canada: Athabasca University Press. Retrieved from http://www.aupress.ca/index.php/books/120233.

Zawacki-Richter, O., Kondakci, Y., Bedenlier, S., Alturki, U., Aldraiweesh, A., & Püplichhuysen, D. (2015). The development of distance education systems in Turkey, the Russian Federation and Saudi Arabia. *European Journal of Open, Distance and E-Learning, 18*(2), 113–128.

Australia

Colin Latchem

Introduction

The chapter describes the history of open and distance learning in Australian higher education, and its transition from the margins to mainstream with a growing number of university students undertaking online and other external modes without ever having actually set foot on a campus.

Australian Distance Education from the 1900s to the 1980s

The goal of public education in Australia has always been equality of opportunity for all students, regardless of their geographic, social or economic circumstances. Blainey (1966) describes how, with a widely distributed population occupying the world's largest island continent, 'the tyranny of distance' has shaped Australia's people, institutions and ideas. One third of Australia's 23,783,500 people live in rural and regional Australia. They contribute two-thirds of Australia's export earnings but on average, they pay five times much as metropolitan residents to access such essential services as hospitals, schools, colleges and universities. Regional students remain under-represented in higher education A third of the university students are from urban centres, while 12.7% are from the inner regional areas, 12.5% from the outer regional areas and only 7% from the remote areas (McKenzie 2016). Therefore, it is hardly surprising that Australia has pioneered distance learning to try to equalise educational opportunities. However, it is not only those in the 'outback' who turn to

C. Latchem (✉)
Open learning consultant, Perth, WA, Australia
e-mail: clatchem@iinet.net.au

© The Author(s) 2018
A. Qayyum and O. Zawacki-Richter (eds.), *Open and Distance Education in Australia, Europe and the Americas*, SpringerBriefs in Open and Distance Education, https://doi.org/10.1007/978-981-13-0298-5_2

distant study. Many students in the urban areas lead complex lives and face competing priorities and so opt for the convenience and flexibility of this mode.

Australian distance education has gone through three phases:

1. Correspondence/external studies, largely by means of mail and lacking direct student interaction with the teacher (1910–1970s).
2. Distance education, using multi-media and two-way communication to improve the effectiveness of the teaching and learning (early 1970s to mid-1980s).
3. Open, flexible and online learning, using the internet and digital technologies and providing increased student-teacher/student-student interaction, collaborative group work and flexibility for the learners (mid-1980s to the present day).

External studies were first offered in response to demands from politically influential rural graziers for more convenient and less costly access to university education. The University of Queensland's inaugural charter of 1909 committed the university to such provision and in 1911[1] UQ became the first university in the southern hemisphere and one of the first in the world to offer degree-level external studies (Cunningham et al. 1997).[2] Largely in response to political pressure from non-metropolitan electorates, The Royal Melbourne Institute of Technology began offering external studies in 1919, followed by the University of Western Australia in 1921 (Guiton and Smith 1984).

Following WWII, universities such as Sydney and Melbourne enabled service and ex-service personnel to study by external means but as Northcott (1984) observed, there were concerns about the academic credibility of this mode of study. For example, in 1951 the Professional Board of the University of Sydney concluded that:

> External studies are necessarily greatly inferior to internal studies and even with the most carefully organised and well staffed external department so little could be achieved, and that so imperfectly, that the establishment of external studies cannot be recommended.

The view in what became known as 'dual-mode universities' was that distance teaching was best provided by academics within the teaching departments rather than within external studies departments. However, in 1949, a desire to improve the quality of distance provision led UQ to make its division of external studies an academic department in its own right with specialists recruited to write and service external courses closely linked to those on campus. However, UQ's 3000 external students proved too small a base for operating in this way, and no other Australian university adopted this model (White 1982; Store and Chick 1982).

1954 saw another newcomer to external studies: the new rural university, University of New England, in the small New South Wales town of Armidale. The need to

---

[1] Secondary level correspondence education for school children began in 1909 in the state of Victoria and in 1914 at primary level. Other states soon followed. The famous School of the Air was born when it was realised that outback children were all taught to use the Royal Flying Doctor Service radios and that that this network could be used to broadcast school lessons. In 2005, there were more than sixteen schools of the air located around Australia. New digital means of teaching and learning are constantly being incorporated into the schools of the air.

[2] By 1910, correspondence courses for teachers were also on offer (Stacey 2005).

attract sufficient numbers of students to and ensure that the external courses upheld the reputation of the university, led UNE to pioneer a model of dual-mode studies that came to influence many institutions throughout Australia and the world:

1. The requirement that full-time academic staff teach both internal and external students concurrently in the same courses.
2. An emphasis on face-to-face contact between staff and students and students and students through residential and week-end schools.
3. The establishment of a Department of External Studies as a service unit for both students and staff (Eastcott and Small 1984).

The Murray Report of 1957[3] unequivocally supported external studies, saying:

> We are convinced that there is a definite need in Australia for universities to be given on a part-time and on an external basis. In particular, we think external courses have an important service to perform for many teachers who live in country districts. (para 108)

The professionalism of those involved in distance education and their willingness to reach out to others in the region was reflected in the formation of the Australian and South Pacific External Studies Association (ASPESA) in 1973 (now the Open and Distance Learning Association of Australia[4]), the initiation of biennial ASPESA forums, and the publication of the peer-reviewed journal *Distance Education* in 1980.[5]

By 1981 there were 13 universities providing external courses across the nation and recognised by the Tertiary Education Commission:

Queensland:

Capricornia Institute of Advanced Education, Rockhampton (later Central Queensland University). The University of Queensland, Brisbane.

Darling Downs Institute of Advanced Education, Toowoomba (later University of Southern Queensland).

New South Wales:

The University of New England, Armidale.

Macquarie University, Sydney.

Mitchell College of Advanced Education, Bathurst (later Charles Sturt University).

Riverina College of Advanced Education, Wagga Wagga (later a campus of Charles Sturt University).   .

---

[3]This first national and wide-ranging investigation of Australian university education by the Committee on Australian Universities in heralded the beginning of government influence on higher education. It revealed acute inadequacies in the standard of university education and recommended increased expenditure so that universities were not only for the privileged few, and the formation of a Universities Grants Committee (see http://www.voced.edu.au/content/ngv%3A53782).

[4]https://odlaa.org/.

[5]http://www.tandfonline.com/loi/cdie20#.VmzbZkp96Uk. This was one of the first journals ever published focusing exclusively on research in the fields of open, distance and flexible education and it remains a primary source of scholarly work in these fields.

Victoria:

Deakin University, Geelong.
Warrnambool Institute of Advanced Education, Warrnambool (later a campus of Deakin University).
Gippsland Institute of Advanced Education, Churchill (later a campus of Monash University).
Royal Melbourne Institute of Technology, Melbourne (later RMIT University).

Western Australia:

Murdoch University, Perth.
Western Australian Institute of Technology, Perth (later Curtin University).

This growth was in response to a more competitive labour market; increased community interest in lifelong learning and upgrading qualifications; increased numbers of older students attracted to external study; increased concern for the education of women with families, disabled persons and other groups; improvements in the quality of courses, tuition and study facilities; and the need of some institutions to attract external students in order to maintain their total enrolments.

Concerns about the proliferation of external studies courses led Johnson (1983) and Shott (1983) to recommend a national policy of collaboration and co-ordination to ensure quality and avoid duplication and gaps in provision. The Commonwealth government had now assumed full responsibility for higher education funding and a federal election in 1987 saw a new Labor government accepting the Commonwealth Tertiary Education Commission (1986) recommendation to limit the number of providers to six (later expanded to eight) specialist Distance Education Centres (DECs) funded to raise the quality of distance education provision and collaborate with non-DECs whose role was limited to delivery. However, in 1993, recognition that there was more to distance education than pre-packaged learning, and growing interest in distance learning in many other institutions led to the abandonment of the DEC monopoly, enabling all institutions to offer courses by whatever means they wished (Johnson 1996; Stacey 2005).

Australian Distance, Open, Flexible and Online Education from the 1980s to the Present Day

At the time of writing, Australia's 40 public universities, two international universities and one private university (See Annex) were serving 1,410,133 students (1,046,682 domestic and 363,451 overseas) (Australian Government Department of Education and Training 2016, 2017a, b). Under both Labour and conservative Liberal-National Coalition governments, university funding has been reduced, study costs have been transferred from the state to the individual, there have been increasing calls for quality assurance and accountability and the universities have had to compete nationally and internationally for their students. The institutions have therefore had to ensure that their courses and services are client-responsive, cost effective and innovative and this has led them all to adopt forms of open, distance and online learning.

The use of blended and digital learning solutions blurs the boundaries between conventional on-campus education and distance education. The Federal Department of Education and Training's national statistics[6] do not include distance education as a separate category but they do record off-campus and mixes of on-and off-campus enrolments and show that online is now the dominant form of off-campus delivery. Most universities have some online enrolments, but the six regional universities are the major off-campus providers, teaching more than three-quarters of their students off-campus. Charles Sturt University in regional New South Wales is the largest off-campus provider, serving 29,000 students. The other major providers are the University of Southern Queensland (18,000 off-campus students), University of New England (over 17,000 students), Deakin University in Melbourne (13,000 distance students), Central Queensland University (9400 students) and The University of Tasmania with (8700 students). The majority of students at Charles Darwin University, serving Darwin and the Northern Territory's tropical and desert regions, are studying at a distance and one third of the students at Southern Cross University serving the north coast of New South Wales and southern Gold Coast in Queensland study by these means.

In the last decade, the proportion of domestic students studying externally[7] has increased from 21 to 25%, or 29% if the private Open Universities Australia (OUA) consortium (described later in the chapter) is included. The increase has been in postgraduate, 'multi-modal'[8] and OUA courses rather than in undergraduate courses in the public universities. Part-time and older students are more likely than full-time school leavers to take at least some of their courses off-campus. It is estimated that about 60% of the students are enrolled in courses that have the potential to be wholly online. Education and postgraduate courses make greatest use of off-campus study. Business and IT courses which would seem to lend themselves to online study have only mid-range levels of off-campus enrolment. Architecture, science, engineering and creative arts are the fields where off-campus study is the least common.

Insert chart with the development of enrolments here.

There has been a decline in the number of international (mainly Asian) students studying off-campus—from 24,000 in 2004 to 11,000 in 2011. This is largely due to Asian families regarding on-campus study as "real university education" and on-campus attendance being obligatory for some degrees, especially at advanced

---

[6]http://highereducationstatistics.education.gov.au/.

[7]Where lesson materials, assignments, etc. are delivered to the student and any associated attendance at the institution is of an incidental, irregular, special or voluntary nature.

[8]Where study is undertaken both on and off campus.

level and changes to migration rules in 2003[9] Expatriates now account for much of this market (Norton et al. 2013; Innovative Research Universities 2013).

The universities are adopting more flexible and multi-modal study and enabling students to embark on their studies whenever they are ready and to gain their qualifications more quickly (Online Study Australia 2015). Examples include Monash University offering mixed-mode postgraduate courses and research degrees with six intakes and six-week teaching periods throughout the year, Swinburne University's Swinburne Online enabling students to fit their study schedule and workloads around life and work, and Curtin University's Curtin Online, whose study options include undergraduate postgraduate and OUA courses and MOOCs. The University of Queensland is but one institution embracing the "flipped classroom model". In the psychology course, The Science of Everyday Thinking, online lectures are viewed as homework, and class time is used for discussion, problem-solving and challenging students in their learning (Norton et al. op cit).

Lecture Capture

Lecture capture has become pervasive in Australian universities, student demand being the primary driver. It helps students who have scheduling difficulties, are unfamiliar with the language, terminology or concepts, or would like to review the content. Evidence suggests that students who don't attend class and access lecture recordings perform better than students who neither attend lectures or access lecture recordings and students from non-English speaking backgrounds and with disabilities and medical conditions gain specific benefits from this but the size of the impacts is not very large, in part because lectures are just one element of students' learning experience (McGrath 2015). Sankey (2013) concluded that while lecture capture was popular with students it was in danger of increasing their workload and encouraging passive learning and that the use of short videos in flipped classroom contexts might be a more effective way of scaffolding the learning.

Open Universities Australia

A report to the Universities Commission (Committee on Open University 1975) rejected the concept of an open university for Australia, due largely to opposition by the existing distance education providers and its recommendations for a national

---

[9]Many international students dream of staying in Australia after they have completed their studies. However, to meet the General Skilled Migration requirements administered by the Department of Immigration and Border Protection and driven by the labour market needs of Australia depends upon applicants' scores in the Points Test. One of the requirements is that applicants have obtained an Australian qualification in Australia (excluding online or distance study) as a result of at least two years of study.

institute of open tertiary education to stimulate innovation were never adopted. But in 1992, Open Learning Australia (OLA) was launched to meet the needs of the large number of students with diverse backgrounds, qualifications, motivations and capacities for higher education study who seemingly could not gain access by conventional means. Initially funded and supported by the Federal Government, the OLA grew out of an earlier TV Open Learning Project pioneered by Monash University, some partner universities and the Australian Broadcasting Corporation. It was not an open university granting its own degrees, but a private educational broker which waived matriculation, had no quotas, provided special preparatory and bridging programmes and operated credit transfer and credit accumulation systems that enabled learners wishing to do so to graduate from the conventional universities of their choice (Latchem and Pritchard 1994; King 1993). In its first four years, it attracted over 30,000 students who would not otherwise have had access to university study.

Today, renamed as Open Universities Australia (OUA)[10] this for-profit consortium which is owned by seven public universities—Curtin, Griffith, Macquarie, Monash, RMIT University, Swinburne and the University of South Australia—and 14 other higher or vocational education providers provide open entry units which do not require any academic entry requirements. At the time of writing, OUA offers 1000 online units and more than 156 qualifications in arts and humanities, business, education, health, information technology, law and justice, and science and engineering provided by 12 of Australia's leading universities. The students pay a fee for 13-week units of undergraduate study (half the cost of a semester's study through a conventional university). The collaborating universities offer degree pathways and by successfully completing a number of units (24 in the case of most of the bachelor's degrees) graduates become eligible to graduate with a full qualification.

OUA's services include Smartthinking, a free 24/7 service providing tutorial and advisory services, feedback on assignments or drafts, and a learning analytics system tracking individual learners' progress. Studies suggest that OUA's costs per student place are about half those of the public universities (Norton et al. 2013). Since 1993, OUA has enabled nearly half a million students to achieve their educational and career goals, but having demonstrated the educational and commercial potential of open learning for the learning cohort of 25 years and over, it faced competition from Australian, Asian, US and European universities and corporate entities and so transformed itself into an online provider across the whole of the tertiary sector. In 2013, it launched Open2Study, a teaching, learning and assessment platform which enables universities to offer free courses online and compete with global online learning platform providers such as Coursera and EdX. The learning platform consists of self-contained interactive weekly modules which are completed over a four-week period with online multiple-choice assessments at the end of each module, at the end of which students scoring 60% across the four test for each course receive a completion certificate. In 2013, it also acquired a 100% interest in Interact Learning Pty Ltd., trading as e3Learning, an Australian online training and compliance provider for corporate customers in Australia, New Zealand and the UK and launched the Open

---

[10]https://www.open.edu.au.

Training Institute, a Registered Training Organisation (RTO) offering online Vocational Education and Training (VET). In 2015, OUA had 45,065 students enrolled in 126,361 units, aged 13–95 (68% 30 and over) from 107 countries and despite the sector undergoing enormous change and plateauing enrolments for the first time since the Federal Government introduced the demand-driven system and competition from the universities, it managed to achieve a modest growth in students number and record a net profit (OUA 2016).

OER

Australian universities have been at the forefront of promoting the use of open education resources (OER). Charles Sturt University, University of Tasmania and University of Technology and the Australian Government Department of Education and Training (Student Information and Learning Branch) Higher Education Group have developed a National Roadmap to support policies for the (re)use and production of open education resources (OER), promote innovative pedagogical models, and respect and empower learners as co-producers in their lifelong learning. It has sourced 22 case studies and drafted 25 strategies to demonstrate the benefits of developing and using OER and need for a national strategy to leverage their use to improve the productivity of higher education.[11]

The University of Southern Queensland (USQ) made an early commitment to OER by offering 10 of its courses to the MIT Open CourseWare Consortium (now the Open Education Consortium) in 2007. Since that time, USQ has encouraged the use of OER in its programmes, joined international partnerships to share open courses and content globally and allowed its materials to repurposed and reused by other Australian and US universities, Australian TAFE Colleges, and other providers. USQ was also a founding anchor partner of the global Open Educational Resources universitas (OERu)[12] and continues to contribute open courses for credit.

MOOCs

For all the criticisms of massive open online courses (MOOCs), their rise signals that people want to learn in very different ways. Recognising this, Australian universities are developing their own MOOCs, some of which institutions including the Australian National University, Monash University and University of Queens-

---

[11] http://openedoz.org/resources/.
[12] https://oeru.org/.

land are contributing to some of the global MOOC platforms. Others, including Queensland University of Technology, University of New South Wales, and Swinburne University, have added their MOOCs to the OUA's Open2Study (The Good Universities Guide 2016).

U3A Online

Social isolation, particularly for the older members of the community and people with disabilities, can be demoralising. One organisation that is well aware of this is the University of the Third Age (U3A), an international movement that provides low cost, informal lifelong learning for millions of retired people around the world. No prior qualifications are necessary and no degrees are awarded.

In 1998, U3A ACT in Canberra and U3A groups in New Zealand considered the possibility of an Internet-based project for the UN International Year of the Older Person. To meet the costs of this initiative, these groups partnered with Griffith University in Queensland and Adult Learning Australia Inc. And since no-one had any knowledge of how to organise virtual courses for older persons unfamiliar with using the Internet, assistance was also sought from the University of Canberra's Faculty of Education, and a Canberra-based Internet enterprise was appointed to host the website. In June 1999, U3A Online Inc.[13]—the world's first virtual University of the Third Age - began offering online courses and basic computing skills for the elderly and disabled in homes, aged care facilities and retirement villages across the nation. U3A Online is incorporated in NSW as a non-profit association and its website is hosted by Griffith University in Brisbane. Its online courses are developed by volunteer subject writers and editors, accessible throughout the year, and studied independently or with the guidance of volunteer course leaders.

Universities are also increasingly offering informal online courses. For example, the University of Western Australia's UWA Extension offers fee-for-service six-week interactive courses in conjunction with the global virtual college, Education to Go. The learners work through tutorials, take quizzes, complete assignments and participate in discussions with their fellow students and instructors. Those receiving over 64% in their final multiple choice exam receive an Online Certificate.

Accreditation and Quality Assurance

Australia's universities are self-accrediting and have a reasonably high level of autonomy to operate within the legislative requirements associated with their Australian Government funding. The Tertiary Education Quality Assurance Agency (TEQSA)[14]

---

[13]https://www.u3aonline.org.au/home.
[14]http://www.teqsa.gov.au/about.

registers and evaluates the performance of higher education providers against the Higher Education Standards Framework (Threshold Standards) 2015, which all providers must meet in order to enter and remain within Australia's higher education system.

The Australian Council of Open and Distance Education (ACODE)[15] has designed eight benchmarks for continuous improvement and quality assurance in technology-enhanced learning, which ACODE (p6) suggests "is now mission critical within higher education institutions for the quality delivery of courses and programs". These benchmarks can be used by institutions, service areas or units within institutions, and collaboratively with other institutions. They concern eight dimensions:

1. Institution-wide policy and governance for technology enhanced learning.
2. Planning for institution-wide quality improvement of technology enhanced learning.
3. Information technology systems, services and support for technology enhanced learning.
4. The application of technology enhanced learning services.
5. Staff professional development for the effective use of technology enhanced learning.
6. Staff support for the use of technology enhanced learning.
7. Student training for the effective use of technology enhanced learning.
8. Student support for the use of technology enhanced learning.

Each dimension involves a Scoping Statement, a Good Practice Statement, a set of Performance Indicators (PIs) and a section for entering recommendations for improvement after self-assessment. Institutions may also formulate their own PIs. Each PI comprises Performance Measures, each of which is rated on a 5-point scale (level 5 indicates good practice). There are also five statements that represent progress toward good practice (as represented by an indicator). ACODE explains that it is not necessary to aspire to best practice in all eight dimensions to establish where an institution sits in relation to other universities (ACODE 2014).

The findings from a 24 university study regarding the fitness for purpose of the ACODE Benchmarks and the benchmarking exercise activities show that they need minor modifications to generate useful quality assurance information but that

---

[15] See: http://www.acode.edu.au/. An organisation of Australasian universities, ACODE's mission is to enhance policy and practice in open distance and e-learning in Australasian higher education by:

- disseminating and sharing knowledge and expertise;
- supporting professional development and providing networking opportunities;
- investigating, developing and evaluating new approaches;
- advising and influencing key bodies in higher education; and
- promoting best practice.

they represent a robust approach to benchmarking and can assist higher education institutions in meeting their regulatory compliance obligations and should be used to inform QA agencies and be embedded within their standards and/or practices (Sankey and Padró 2015).

What Is the Future for Australian Distance Education?

With globalisation and measured progress of change being replaced with an explosion of new and unforseen ideas and developments such as MOOCs and online start-ups in search of revenue changing student demographics and societal expectations, ever-increasing costs and reducing government funding, Australian universities,[16] will need to consider how respond to and extract maximum value and benefits from the various forms of distance education. PwC and Australian Higher Education Industrial Association (2016) claim that the introduction of new technology and new devices familiar to the students into universities is challenging the traditional on campus experience, lowering the barriers to entry for new and differentiated tertiary education providers and providing new revenue streams, competition and disruption. They also suggest that to remain relevant and competitive the universities will need to maintain their inherent advantages while embracing the ways in which digital technologies can transform and improve the ways in which their courses are delivered and accessed.

With Australian Government Department of Education and Training (2017a, b) releasing its latest data on completion rates at Australian universities, The Conversation (2017) points to the fact that in years past, students were typically 18 years old, middle-class, child-free and otherwise unencumbered school-leavers who often received financial support from their families for university study. Today, the students who study off campus are typically part-time, older, from working class, indigenous or disadvantaged backgrounds or regional areas of Australia—and less likely to complete their courses. While a large number of students (670,000) are in the 18–22 years age bracket, latest available figures from 2015 show there were over 181,000 students aged 30–39; almost 90,000 aged 40–49; over 36,000 aged 50–59; and almost 10,000 aged 60 and over, a growing number of whom never actually set foot on campus. Many dip in and out of study, some change programmes or even universities and some take almost a decade to complete their three-year degree, and rural and regional students tend to take longer than metropolitan and higher socio-economic status students to complete their studies. They lead complex lives and have to manage

---

[16]To be classified as universitities in Australia, organisations must meet set criteria as governed by Commonwealth Government Provider Category. The most restrictive of these is the requirement to be active in research 'across at least three broad fields of study: disciplines such as health, engineering, education or science'. In mid- 2014 there were 172 higher education providers operating in Australia of which only 40 of these were classified as universities. The remainder of these providers are classified as nonuniversity higher education providers (NUHEP) comprised of both private and publicly listed organisations, largely with a focus on teaching only and often providing specialist or vocationally focused courses (PwC and AHEIA 2016).

competing priorities, including paid employment while studying. They lack familiarity with university life and expectations and this means they need special personal and academic support and mechanisms for measuring, monitoring and responding to their attrition rates.

From the other available evidence, it would appear that:

- Political agendas, commercial imperatives, the requirement to provide evidence of quality in outputs, outcomes and impacts and technology innovation will continue to be the main drivers of change.
- With the proliferation of public, private and online providers, the universities will have ensure that they use digitisation to enhance learning experiences and improve outcomes rather than for the purposes of cost cutting or profit.
- Many students are likely to still want the on-campus experience but the roll-out of Australia's National Broadband Network and a generation of students well used to ICT and online study, work and collaboration is likely bring about a growing demand for online learning.
- Uses of technology will affect student choices between education providers and so the institutions will need to ensure that their teaching and learning is accessible, equitable, student-focused, flexible, affordable and informed by the latest theories and practices.
- The universities will need to capitalise on the potential of online learning in their international (particularly Asian) markets. In 2015, The total export income generated by all international education activity (spending by onshore students and offshore earning from other educational services) was $19.4 billion, making this Australia's third biggest export and largest services export industry. Of this total, higher education generated $12.9 billion (Australian Government Department of Education and Training 2016).
- With the growing demand for lifelong, lifewide learning, the universities will need to find ways of providing more nonformal and formal learning for mature students, using prior learning assessment and recognition, free or low-cost short online introductory courses, credit transfer and learning pathways linking informal/nonformal learning to degree-level studies.
- To remain at the cutting edge, reduce costs, diversify, and be competitive, the universities will need to share their knowledge, skills and resources with other higher education institutions, the corporate sector and others in the developed and developing world.

Acknowledgements The author acknowledges the suggestions and advice offered by Ms. Julie Hare, Higher Education Editor, *The Australian* and Dr. Som Naidu, President of ODLAA and editor of *Distance Education*.

Annex: List of Australian Universities

Australian Capital Territory

- Australian National—http://www.anu.edu.au/
- University of Canberra—http://www.canberra.edu.au/

New South Wales

- Australian Catholic University—https://www.acu.edu.au/
- Charles Sturt University—http://www.csu.edu.au/
- Macquarie University—https://www.mq.edu.au/
- Southern Cross University—http://scu.edu.au/
- University of New England—https://www.une.edu.au/
- University of New South Wales—http://www.international.unsw.edu.au/
- University of Newcastle—https://www.newcastle.edu.au/
- University of Sydney—http://sydney.edu.au/
- University of Technology, Sydney—http://www.uts.edu.au/
- Western Sydney University—http://www.westernsydney.edu.au/
- University of Wollongong—https://www.uow.edu.au/

Northern Territory

- Charles Darwin University—http://www.cdu.edu.au/
- Bond University—http://bond.edu.au/
- CQ University—https://www.cqu.edu.au/
- Griffith University—http://www.griffith.edu.au/
- James Cook University—http://www.jcu.edu.au/
- Queensland University of Technology—https://www.qut.edu.au/
- University of Queensland—http://www.uq.edu.au/
- University of Southern Queensland—http://www.usq.edu.au/
- University of the Sunshine Coast—http://www.usc.edu.au/

South Australia

- Carnegie Mellon University—http://www.australia.cmu.edu/
- Flinders University—http://www.flinders.edu.au/
- Torrens University Australia—http://www.torrens.edu.au/
- University College London—http://www.ucl.ac.uk/australia
- University of Adelaide—http://international.adelaide.edu.au/
- University of South Australia—http://www.unisa.edu.au

Tasmania

- University of Tasmania—http://www.utas.edu.au/

Victoria

- Deakin University—http://www.deakin.edu.au/
- Federation University of Australia—http://federation.edu.au/

- La Trobe University—http://www.latrobe.edu.au/
- Monash University—https://www.monash.edu/
- RMIT University—https://www.rmit.edu.au/
- Swinburne University of Technology—http://www.swinburne.edu.au/
- University of Divinity—http://www.divinity.edu.au/
- University of Melbourne—http://www.unimelb.edu.au/
- Victoria University—http://www.vu.edu.au/

Western Australia

- Curtin University—http://www.curtin.edu.au/
- Edith Cowan University—http://www.ecu.edu.au/
- Murdoch University—http://www.murdoch.edu.au/
- University of Notre Dame Australia—http://www.nd.edu.au/
- University of Western Australia—http://www.international.uwa.edu.au/

References

ACODE. (2014). *Benchmarks for technology enhanced learning.* Canberra, ACT: Australasian Council on Open, Distance and e-learning (ACODE). http://www.acode.edu.au/pluginfile.php/579/mod_resource/content/3/TEL_Benchmarks.pdf.

Australian Government Department of Education and Training. (2016). *Export income to Australia from international education activity in 2015.* Canberra, ACT: Australian Government Department of Education and Training https://internationaleducation.gov.au/research/Research-Snapshots/Documents/Export%20Income%20CY2015.pdf.

Australian Government Department of Education and Training. (2017a). *Completion rates of higher education students: Cohort analysis, 2005–2014.* Canberra, ACT: Australian Government Department of Education and Training. https://docs.education.gov.au/system/files/doc/other/cohort_analysis_2005-2014_0.pdf.

Australian Government Department of Education and Training. (2017b). *uCube—Higher education statistics.* Canberra, ACT: Australian Government Department of Education and Training. http://highereducationstatistics.education.gov.au/Default.aspx.

Blainey, G. (1966). *The tyranny of distance: How distance shaped Australia's history.* Melbourne, VIC: Sun Books.

Committee on Open University. (1975). *Open tertiary education in Australia: Final report of the Committee on Open University to the Universities Commission, December 1974 (The Karmel Report).* Canberra, ACT: Australian Government Publishing Service. file:///C:/Users/Admin/Downloads/Report%20(1).pdf.

Commonwealth Tertiary Education Commission (Australia) (CTEC). (1986). *Review of efficiency and effectiveness in higher education [Hudson Report].* Canberra, ACT: Australian Government Publishing Service.

Cunningham, S., Tapsall, S., Ryan, Y., Stedman, L., Bagdon, K., & Flew, T. (1997). *New media and borderless education: A review of the convergence between global media networks and higher education provision.* Canberra, ACT: Australian Government Publishing Service, Department of Employment, Education, Training and Youth Affairs, Higher Education Division, Evaluations and Investigations Program.

Eastcott, L. & Small, I. (1984). New South Wales: Getting the mixture right. In K. Smith (Ed.), *Diversity down under in distance education* (pp. 63–67). Australian and South Pacific External Studies Association. Toowoomba: Darling Down Institute Press.

Guiton, P., & Smith, M. (1984). Progress in partnership: External studies in Western Australia. In K. Smith (Ed.), *Diversity down under in distance education* (pp. 83–87). Australian and South Pacific External Studies Association. Toowoomba: Darling Down Institute Press.

Innovative Research Universities. (2013). IRU submission: Coalition's Online Higher Education Working Group. Submission by Charles Darwin University; Flinders University; Griffith University; James Cook University; La Trobe University; Murdoch University; and The University of Newcastle. http //www.iru.edu.au/media/40504/iru%20submission%20to%20coalition% 20online%20learning%20working%20group%20web.pdf.

Johnson, R. (1983). *The Provision of External Studies in Australian Higher Education (Evaluations and investigations program)*. Canberra, ACT: Commonwealth Tertiary Education Commission. http://vital.new.voced.edu.au/vital/access/manager/Repository/ngv:9494/SOURCE2.

Johnson, R. (1996). To wish and to will: Reflections on policy formation and implementation. In T. D. Evans & D. E. Nation (Eds.), *Opening education: Policies and practices from distance education* (pp. 90–102). London: Routledge.

King, B. (1993). Open learning in Australia: Government intervention and institutional response. *Open Learning, 8*(3), 13–25.

Latchem, C., & Pritchard, T. (1994). Open learning: The unique Australian option. *Open Learning, 9*(3), 18–26.

McGrath, D. (2015). *Questions about: Lecture recording*. An occasional paper prepared by the Institute for Teaching and Learning Innovation. August 25, 2015. Brisbane, QLD: Institute for Teaching and Learning Innovation, University of Queensland. https://itali.uq.edu.au/filething/get/3090/LectureRecording-updated.pdf.

McKenzie, B. (2016). Regional students need better access to Australian universities. *The Australian*. January 13, 2016. http://www.theaustralian.com.au/higher-education/opinion/regional-students-need-better-access-to-australian-universities/news-story/6a35ecc68bcac21bb28e2940d201fc2e.

Northcott, P. (1984). The tyranny of distance and proximity. In K. Smith (Ed.), *Diversity down under in distance education* (pp. 39–50). Australian and South Pacific External Studies Association. Toowoomba: Darling Down Institute Press.

Norton, A., Sonnemann, J., & McGannon, C. (2013). *The online evolution: When technology meets tradition in higher education*. Carlton, VIC: Grattan Institute. http://grattan.edu.au/wp-content/uploads/2014/04/186_online_higher_education.pdf.

Online Study Australia. (2015). *Australian distance education universities*. Chapman, ACT: Online Study Australia. https://onlinestudyaustralia.com/best-distance-universities.html.

OUA. (2016). *Open universities Australia—2015 year in review*. Melbourne, VIC: Open Universities Australia. https://www.open.edu.au/yearinreview2015/#welcome-page.

PwC, & AHEIA. (2016). *Australian higher education workforce of the future*. Melbourne, VIC: PwC and Australian Higher Education Industrial Association. https://www.aheia.edu.au/cms_uploads/docs/aheia-higher-education-workforce-of-the-future-report.pdf.

Sankey, M. (2013). *Lecture capture in Australasian universities*. Canberra, ACT: Australasian Council on Open, Distance and e-learning (ACODE). http://www.acode.edu.au/pluginfile.php/419/mod_resource/content/1/ACODE_Lecture_Capture_Report_2013.pdf.

Sankey, M., & Padró, F. (2015). *ACODE benchmarks for Technology Enhanced Learning (TEL): Findings from a 24 university benchmarking exercise regarding the benchmarks' fitness for purpose and capacity to generate useful quality assurance information*. Poster session presentation at 2015 INQAAHE Biennial Conference, 1 April 2015, Chicago, IL, https://eprints.usq.edu.au/28689/3/Sankey%20Padro%2018%20QMOD%20paper%5B2%5D%5B1%5D.pdf.

Shott, M. (1983). External studies in Australia at the crossroads? *ASPESA Newsletter, 9*(2), 2–9.

Stacey, E. (2005). The history of distance education in Australia. *Quarterly Review of Distance Education, 6*(3), 252–259.

Store, R., & Chick, J. (1982). Reaching out in Queensland: A decentralised approach. In K. Smith (Ed.), *Diversity down under in distance education* (pp. 57–67). Australian and South Pacific External Studies Association. Toowoomba: Darling Down Institute Press.

TEQSA. (undated). *TEQSA guidance note benchmarking*. Canberra, ACT: Tertiary Education Quality and Standards Agency (TEQSA). http://www.teqsa.gov.au/sites/default/files/BenchmarkingGNFinal_0.pdf.

The Conversation. (2017). The typical university student is no longer 18, middle-class and on campus—We need to change thinking on "drop-outs". *The Conversation*. February 27, 2017. http://theconversation.com/the-typical-university-student-is-no-longer-18-middle-class-and-on-campus-we-need-to-change-thinking-on-drop-outs-73509.

The Good Universities Guide. (2016). Free online courses (MOOCs). http://www.gooduniversitiesguide.com.au/Support-Centre/Free-Online-Courses-MOOCs#.Vt1DcPl96Um.

White, M.A. (1982). Distance education in Australian higher education–a history. *Distance Education, 3*(2), 255–278.

Australia—Commentary

Som Naidu

Distance education in Australia around the turn of the 20th century was a distinctly different mode of learning and teaching. And as Colin Latchem points out in his contribution to this volume, it was intended for a distinctly different group of learners who lived very far away from large urban centers and removed from where the bulk of the educational institutions were located. It was an alternative solution to educational opportunity, and as such its learning and teaching methods were different from what was conventional practice in face-to-face campus-based educational contexts at the time, appropriately devoid of the thrills and frills of the campus-based educational experience. This alternative solution to learning and teaching had several remarkable attributes which have, over the years, gradually found their way into campus-based educational practice. Foremost among these attributes is the very public nature of the operation. In this mode, unlike what usually occurs within the four walls of a classroom, all communication between the teachers and the learners is out in the open. And because of this exposure, the distance education course material is subjected to higher standards in terms of the design of the instructional transaction it embodies.

The Race to the Center, Can the Enter Hold?

It is now not uncommon to see campus-based education in Australia adopting and integrating many of these attributes as part of their armory of learning and teaching strategies and there are many reasons for this. The first is the increasing adoption of technology to mediate the teaching and learning process. If you consider the textbook and the printed resource as a technology, then technology has always been at the

S. Naidu (✉)
The University of the South Pacific, Suva, Fiji
e-mail: sommnaidu@gmail.com

© The Author(s) 2018
A. Qayyum and O. Zawacki-Richter (eds.), *Open and Distance Education in Australia, Europe and the Americas*, SpringerBriefs in Open and Distance Education,
https://doi.org/10.1007/978-981-13-0298-5_3

heart of the distance education transaction, the affordances of which are naturally very appealing to mainstream educational practices.

But it is not technology alone that is driving this convergence among different modes of learning. The composition of the student population in Australia is changing from the traditional urban and rural divide that characterized the learning group a hundred years ago. The student population is now growing exponentially to include mature age students looking for additional qualifications and on the job-training, stay-home parents looking for career change or enhancement, part-time students, as well as a large body of international students. Another factor that is influencing this change in conventional educational practices is the rising cost of education that is increasingly being shifted on to the consumer. And if the user or the consumer must pay for the services then, it forces institutions to become a lot more innovative in their approaches to teaching and learning, and eliminating as much redundancy as is possible.

While such cross-fertilization between modes augurs well for learning and teaching generally, it has its risks, and these have to do with being able to retain the integrity of a mode while adopting it as a part of mainstream processes. Distance education for instance, and as an alternative mode, was always intended for a very unique educational context. Openness in terms of access, and independence, flexibility and self-direction have been its hallmarks, indeed its threshold principles (Naidu 2016). Increasing transformation of distance education with the integration of technologies which are not time, place and pace independent runs the risk of undermining its integrity, threatening its core threshold principles, and thus failing to serve out its mandate. The remotely located distance learner still exists both in the developed and developing contexts. Along with first-time learners, they include professionals such as doctors, nurses, social workers and school teachers who are working in remote locations, living on a farm, and in a small rural town. They need access to educational opportunities, and not every one of them, even in technologically and economically developed social contexts is flush with the latest tools and connectivity. For them distance learning is critical. They want and need distance education, not online education, not blended learning, nor technology-enhanced education. In fact, they would prefer the leanest and meanest version of it, so that they can get on with their jobs and be able to study as well, without the imposition of the need for constant connectivity.

The Opportunity and the Challenge

The Tertiary Education Quality and Standards Agency in Australia takes the view that there is room for a variety of modes of learning. As one size does not, and will not fit all. This may include campus-based face-to-face education, fully online learning, including MOOCs, blended learning and distance learning. In Australia where there are no single mode dedicated distance education institutions, this makes good sense also because not every skill or subject matter can be taught as effectively and efficiently by any one mode. A wide variety of modes are required to meet the needs of an equally wide variety of learners, skills and subject matter that needs to be learned.

The challenge for Australian educational providers in this space is to be very careful about appropriately matching a mode of learning with the learners it is intended to serve, the skill or subject matter that needs to be learned, while ensuring integrity of practice in terms of its threshold principles. Distance education, flexible learning, and online learning is not business as usual. These alternative modes to teaching and learning require a fundamental shift in perspectives and perceptions about teaching and learning. They require new tools and technologies, and new skill sets across the board. Many of the campus-based providers that are racing to adopt these modes of education, such as in the case of the adoption of MOOCs, do not have these requisite skill sets and resources for effectively engaging in these modes, and falling into the trap of doing a very poor job of it (Baggaley 2016). In this race to the center, adopters of alternative modes of learning and teaching such as distance and online learning are failing to learn from the lessons of their past. Adherence to their threshold principles is important.

References

Baggaley, J. (2016). Reflection: Sandcastle competitions. *Distance Education, 37,* 366–375. https://doi.org/10.1080/01587919.2016.1233052.
Naidu, S. (2016). Mainstreaming open, flexible, and distance learning. In K.-W. Lai, S. Stein, P. Field, & K. Pratt (Eds.), *Our world in your place: 30 years of distance learning and teaching at the University of Otago* (pp. 92–108). Distance Learning Office, University of Otago.

Brazil

Fredric Litto

The History and Past of Distance Education

One cannot fully understand the context in which formal learning began and developed in Brazil without considering its legacy of over three-hundred years as a colony of Portugal. Although Spain initiated higher learning in its colonies in the New World as early as the 16th century, establishing universities and granting the right to publish books (Mexico City in 1539, and Lima, Peru, in 1584) and news-papers (Mexico City, 1541), the Portuguese Crown prohibited all publications and advanced studies in its continental-sized colony until the nineteenth-century, when the Monarch of Portugal, Dom João VI, fleeing Napoleon, moved to Brazil with his court, his library and his printing press in 1808 (Moraes 2013).

Until then, Brazil had been entirely dependent on Portugal's only university, in Coimbra, for the higher learning of its citizens. But Dom João only permitted the creation of four specialized institutions in Brazil: a school for naval engineering in Rio de Janeiro (actually created earlier, in 1782), a medical school in Bahia, a mining school in Minas Gerais, and two law schools, one in Pernambuco, and the other in São Paulo—but no university, because, it was thought, in such institutions the inhabitants *think* and may come to unsettling ideas. Hence, it was only in 1934 that true, multi-school academic establishments came about in three different locations: the (State) University of São Paulo, the (now Federal) University of Paraná, and the (now Federal) University of Rio de Janeiro.

Portuguese conservatism in relation to education continues to this day in Brazil, making innovation and experimentation in pedagogy and curriculum at all levels of learning extremely difficult to carry-out. Even the genial ideas of Brazilian educator Paulo Freire (1921–1997), so highly recognized abroad, tend to remain confined to the

F. Litto (✉)
Brazilian Association of Distance Education, São Paulo, Brazil
e-mail: frmlitto@terra.com.br

© The Author(s) 2018
A. Qayyum and O. Zawacki-Richter (eds.), *Open and Distance Education in Australia, Europe and the Americas*, SpringerBriefs in Open and Distance Education, https://doi.org/10.1007/978-981-13-0298-5_4

halls of teacher-training institutions. And French-influenced educational strategies, placing highly-emphasized importance of abstract thinking on the part of students, and educational theories and ideologies among teachers, is dominant over North American pragmatism, with its inclusion of "hands-on" experience, real collaboration between students, *and* between teaching staff members. Consequently, the role of technology in learning has suffered from multiple obstacles: the low salaries paid to instructors do not attract the strongest and most independent minds to the profession; teacher-training institutions concentrate almost entirely on the theoretical aspects of teaching students, leaving the practical matters of the classroom to happenstance; in the first decades of computers in classrooms, teachers thought it beneath them to familiarize themselves with machines, wires and networks; the Portuguese language is a "minority-language," one spoken by 263 million persons around the world (but almost all of them residing in economically-undistinguished countries) and the amount of open educational resources on the web in the language is not abundant, while English as a working language is very badly taught in schools and not required for study in universities.

Public primary and secondary education was only introduced into Brazil in the first decades of the twentieth century, and even then it served principally the upper and upper-middle classes. Although recent legislation stipulates that primary and secondary school attendance is obligatory for all young people, this requirement is not rigorously observed outside large cities. The country's Constitution of 1988 designated municipal governments as responsible for the supervision and governance of primary education, state governments for secondary learning, and the federal government for tertiary studies. Consequently, it is not surprising that the introduction of distance education came to Brazil at a very late date; and open learning is still trying to find its proper place in the environment.

The Function and Position of Distance Education Within the National Higher Education System

Although there is precarious evidence of distance learning in Brazil at the beginning of the 20th century, with announcements of correspondence courses in subjects like shorthand and the study of languages, later including technical specialities, the use of radio for informal instruction began in 1936, and that of television in 1958 (Alves 2009). In the 1970s, Brazil was one of the world's most celebrated centers of distance-based, pre-university iniciatives, principally because of Project SACI (Advanced Interdisciplinary Communications Satellite) of the National Institute of Space Research (INPE), which had the objective of upgrading the competencies of school teachers of Brazil's Northeast, many of whom taught primary school without having, themselves, finished secondary school; and the Telecurso (initially dedicated to secondary education—later expanded to include primary education—and directed to adults who had missed earlier opportunities for such studies), organized by the

Roberto Marinho Foundation in partnership with large entities of civil society, transmitted by the Globo Television Network, and which continues to the present time (Litto 2011).

The successful initiation of the United Kingdom's Open University in 1970 inspired a group of Brazilian legislators to visit that institution in 1972, after which began a series of attempts to create a similar entity in Brazil, all defeated through discriminatory judgments at various levels: the Legislative Branch of government, the Ministry of Education and even the governance committees of the University of Brasília, the first Brazilian university whose rector actually signed a memorandum of agreement with the UKOU for technical support (Azevedo 2012). Perhaps it was the creation of the Open University of Portugal in 1988 which embarrassed the former colony into taking distance-based university learning more seriously, for in 1992 the Federal University of Mato Grosso began planning the first distance-based correspondence course in teacher-preparation, which actually began with 350 in-service teachers in 1995. By 2005, it was offering full undergraduate programs in Pedagogy at a distance for 2000 teachers, and in 2009 began offering this course to the many Brazilians living in Japan.

In the meantime, the Law of Policies and Bases (LDB) of 1996, which took ten years to elaborate and negotiate to approval through the National Congress, gave new status to distance learning, stating in Article 80 that academic degrees earned through distance means had exactly the same value as those earned through conventional approaches. It stipulated that full, distance-based, masters and doctoral degrees could be offered, and that commercial radio and television channels give specially-reduced costs for transmitting educational content—two measures still not yet completely implanted.

But it took until 2000 for other Federal institutions to receive approval from the Ministry of Education to begin distance learning: the Federal University of Pará for bachelor's degree and *licenciatura* (school teacher's license) in Mathematics and the Federal University of Ceará for *licenciatura* in Biology, Physics, Chemistry and Mathematics. By 2002, 25 institutions had been authorized (16 public and 9 private), and by 2012 150 (80 public and 70 private). In 2016, there were 331 institutions of higher education authorized for distance-based undergraduate learning: 74 public (22.4%) and 257 private (77.6%). They currently offer 1365 undergraduate courses. Institutions authorized to offer distance-based post-graduate programs are 177 in number, and they offer 3935 different courses to a vast continuing-education population. Of the total number of professors active in higher education in Brazil today (383,386), 13,083 (3.4%) are dedicated to distance-based studies. Other characteristics of the professionals who work in distance-based learning in the country can be found in the English-language version of the annual ABED CensoEAD.Br *Analytical Report of Distance Learning in Brazil* (ABED 2015, pp. 75–77).

The Ministry then created a Secretariat of Distance Education which centralized the rapidly expanding activities in this approach to learning from 2004 to 2010; its extinction constituting yet another example of discontinuity characteristic of the public sector in Brazil. In 2006, there finally was established an Open University of Brazil-UAB, the last one to be created among the nations with populations of over one hundred million persons. To circumvent bureaucratic obstacles and academic prejudices, it was neither "open" (admission requires passing an entrance exam just as difficult as that required for entering into the highly competitive Federal campus-based institutions), nor a "university" (it is a "system" or grouping of public institutions of higher education so that it can be tuition-free). Participating institutions, financially supported by the Federal Government, produce the courses and issue the resulting diplomas. In 2013 it had 103 participating institutions, 667 student study-centers (called *polos* in Portuguese) distributed throughout the country (in "partnership" with local municipal governments, which are supposed to furnish "study-centers"—each one a room with ten computers, connected to the web, and a mini-library), and a total of 243,000 students enrolled. Through an agreement with the Ministry of Education of Mozambique, the content of UAB is shared with students in that language-related nation. Since less than one-half of Brazil's 5565 municipalities have any kind of institution of higher education, the UAB and the efforts of private institutions in distance-based learning, are of great strategic importance to Brazil.

The Regulatory Framework, Policies, Accreditation and Quality Assurance in Distance Education

There are over 70,000 laws concerning education at all levels in Brazil, a fact which, if it guaranteed high quality, would be truly significant; but that is not the case. The following paragraphs offer some general lines of development of the place of tertiary distance-based learning in the country. The most recent Federal Constitution dates from 1988 and affirms that education is a social right for all people, must be gratuitous when offered by public bodies, and is open to private initiative, subject to the "authorization, regulation, supervision and evaluation by public authorities." Distance-based learning is considered that which makes use of the resources and technologies of information and communication, offering flexibility in the organization of space and time (learners and instructors in different locations and times), and didactic-pedagogic mediation with regard to the teaching/learning process.

The Law of Policies and Bases (LDB) of 1996 gave the initial authorization for the beginning of distance education programs at the post-secondary level, but when its operational questions were finally published nine years later, it included clauses of both salutary and dubious natures: (a) the academic credits earned through its courses could be transferred to other institutions (implemented); (b) "full" masters and doctoral degrees (*stricto* sensu) could be offered (never implemented appropriately—see more below); (c) partnerships could be established between universities abroad in order to enrich course offerings, subject to Ministry approval (now a rarity after several unsuccessful attempts); and (d) distance-based courses had to have the same duration as campus-based ones (an obvious interference in institutional autonomy). This grudging or reluctant approval of the new entrant into the country's educational environment continues to today.

The National Council of Education (Conselho Nacional da Educação) is Brazil's highest body responsible for the major issues governing the realization of educational matters (Conselho Nacional da Educação 2014). Composed of representatives of Brazilian society chosen by the Minister of Education, it has two principal "chambers," one for policy-making in primary and secondary school studies, and another for that in higher education. The former has its operational arms in the SAEB-National System of Evaluation of Basic Education, and the latter, the SINAES-National System of Evaluation of Higher Education. CONAES-National Commission for Evaluation of Higher Education is the highest collegiate body of SINAES, and its function is to oversee the monitoring of quality in higher education, through the elaboration of measures to guarantee good practices on the part of institutions.

Students concluding secondary school must take the ENEM-National Examination of Secondary Education, a measure of recent date, and which now serves not only as a benchmarking tool for policy-makers, but as well for identifying candidates for entry into the highly-selective public institutions of post-secondary education (almost six million students sat for the test in 2015, in 2000 municipalities throughout the country). Students concluding higher education studies normally sit for the ENADE-National Exam of Student Performance, prepared by the INEP-National Institute of Studies and Research in Education "Anísio Teixeira", which annually carries out tests throughout the national territory in selected academic subjects with about half a million individuals participating in each iteration of the study (Instituto Nacional De Estudos E Pesquisas Educacionais Anísio Teixeira 2014a, b). It is a special pleasure to report that every year since 2007, students who studied through distance-based programs consistently showed "better performance than those who studied conventionally."

The Ministry of Education makes available to private institutions funds which can be lent to students in need of loans to be able to continue their studies under the following programs: ProUni-University for All Program, and FIES-Fund of Student Financing (distance-based students cannot avail themselves of this benefit, perhaps because government fears that since most students who seek such loans are majoring in school teaching careers, the law stipulates that in that case, the loan need not be repaid).

Institutions seeking to offer distance-based courses approved by the Ministry of Education must submit vast documentation, including a Plan of Institutional Development, an Institutional Pedagogical Project, and a Pedagogical Project of Courses. From these documents, there is derived a profile including an evaluation of the proposal: curriculum, student admission numbers and selection policy, continued student evaluation, attendance control, qualifications of the teaching staff, library and laboratory facilities, and partnerships with other entities. The renovation, every five years, of approved status requires similar documentation efforts.

In 2016, a new set of rules (Marco Regulatório) governing distance-based programs was approved, having several positive corrective features: elimination of the earlier requirement of an institution to be approved for campus-based learning before it could solicit authorization for distance-based programs; permission for institutions to share remote study-centers for distance learners for logistic and economic motives (it is estimated to cost about US$25,000.00 to equip each center); the evaluation of distance-based and campus-based programs will hereafter be carried out simultaneously; the long-standing rule limiting to only 20% the distance-based part of those courses *approved as distance-based courses* can now be "flexibilized" if appropriately justified in the documentation submitted for authorization and renewal; INEP and CAPES (the Ministry's agency coordinating post-graduate studies as well as the UAB-Brazilian Open University), will have 120 days to prepare and disseminate the parameters of "quality" for evaluating distance-based programs and for revising the instruments for measurement.

An Overview of Major Distance Education Teaching and Research Institutions

The principal Brazilian source of research concerning distance-based learning are the top-tier universities, public and private, which offer masters and doctoral degrees requiring the elaboration and public defense of a thesis. Almost exclusively of a "qualitative research" nature (as opposed to a "quantitative" approach which measures and analyses practices, attitudes and actions evolved in the offering of open and distance-based learning), these theses sometimes find their way into learned journals and scholarly books (Litto et al. 2005). Listed below are the fifty most important institutions, public and private, authorized to offer distance-based undergraduate programs and to grant traditional academic degrees. They are ranked in order of student enrollments, but the reader should be aware that some private institutions, although listed separately here, are sometimes part of a single corporate holding entity, and hence able to share resources and make use of other collaborative actions. The UAB Open University of Brazil is not listed below because it chooses to be included through the identities and numbers of its component institutions.

An important element of the production of research on distance learning is the Brazilian Association of Distance Education-ABED (www.abed.org.br), a not-for-profit learned society founded in 1995 and including individual and institutional members from the major educational segments of the country (schools, universities, government and corporate continuing education), both public and private. Its annual International Congress of Distance Education attracts about two-thousand participants, and the submission of about 400 research papers (from which some 220 are selected, to be presented orally, for their relevance and significance). Each year, ABED conducts a detailed *Census* of all distance-based learning in the country, both academic and corporative, publishing its results in Portuguese and English, in printed form and digitally on its site. It also publishes a scholarly journal, *Revista Brasileira de Aprendizagem Aberta e a Distância/Brazilian Journal of Open and Distance Learning*, which carries articles in English, Spanish and Portuguese, and can be found on the Association's site. As a catalyst forming a large and diversified community of professionals, ABED actively supports the creation and development of similar national learned societies dedicated to distance learning in countries in both Latin America and Africa (Table 1).

Some Statistics About Student Enrollments in Distance Education Programs and the Funding of Distance Education

The total number of students enrolled in primary and secondary schools in Brazil is 50,545,050 (Pre-Primary 7,295,512; Primary 29,702,498; Secondary 8,376,852; Education of the Young and Adults (primary and secondary-level studies for those beyond the appropriate classroom age) 3,906,877; Vocational Education 1,063,655; Special Needs Education 820,433). The administrative-financial responsibility for this basic level of learning is as follows: Federal 1%; State 37%; Municipal 46%; Private 16%. The responsibility for Vocational Education is: Federal 16%; State 36%; Municipal 2% and Private 46%. The last grouping (Private) is principally represented by the highly-respected systems sustained by obligatory contributions from enterprises in society (although collected by government, it is *not* public money): SENAI/SESI (industry), SENAC/SESC (commerce), SENAR (agriculture), and SENAT (transportation) (MEC/INEP/DEED *Censo de Educação Básica* 2012).

The total number of post-secondary institutions in 2014 was 2386, distributed as follows: Federal 107 (4.5%), State 118 (5.0%), Municipal 73 (3.1%) and Private 2070 (87.4%). There are four basic categories of institutions: universities—multi-school entities (111 public institutions, with a formidable degree of autonomy over their governance, curriculum and long-range strategies; and 84 private institutions, with reduced autonomy over curriculum, ability to grant degrees, and geographic expansion); university centers—multi-department entities with little autonomy (11 public; 136 private); faculties—smaller institutions either dedicated to a reduced curricular scope (medicine, or law, or administration, or teacher-training, among other subjects) and with very reduced autonomy; and federal institutes/centers for technological education (40 public; no private).

The Ministry of Education has to date authorized 177 institutions to offer distance-based, tertiary-level programs. Although 95.8% of the total number of undergraduate courses are campus-based, and distance-based programs are only 4.0% of these, the latter had a growth factor, from 2013 to 2014, of 41.2%, while the former advanced only by 7%. The regional distribution of campus-based and distance-based tertiary institutions is as follows (Fig. 1).

The total number of students enrolled in post-secondary studies at the under-graduate level in 2014 was 7,828,013 (6.486.171 campus-based (82.5%); 1.341.842 distance learners (17.1%). From 2003 to 2014, the overall *growth* of student numbers was as follows: campus-based 66.9%; distance-based 2.588%. In 2014, 190,000 students graduated from distance-based undergraduate programs authorized by the Ministry (Table 2).

Table 1 Leading institutions of undergraduate distance learning in Brazil ranked by size of student enrollments in 2014

Size	Institutions	Private	Public
1	Universidade Norte Do Paraná	310,855	
2	Universidade Anhanguera—Uniderp	150,631	
3	Centro Universitário Internacional	109,385	
4	Universidade Paulista	100,799	
5	Centro Universitário Leonardo Da Vinci	92,484	
6	Universidade Estácio De Sá	68,766	
7	Centro Universitário Uniseb	43,410	
8	Centro Universitário De Maringá—Unicesumar	39,038	
9	Universidade Metropolitana De Santos	32,688	
10	Universidade De Uberaba	19,352	
11	Centro Universitário Claretiano	18,263	
12	Universidade De Santo Amaro	16,882	
13	Universidade Nove De Julho	13,870	
14	Faculdade Educacional Da Lapa	12,674	
15	Universidade Cidade De São Paulo	12,588	
16	Universidade Luterana Do Brasil	12,244	
17	Faculdade De Tecnologia E Ciências	11,941	
18	Universidade Do Sul De Santa Catarina	10,753	
19	Centro Universitário Da Grande Dourados	9595	
20	Universidade De Franca	9516	
21	Universidade Federal Do Piauí		9110
22	Universidade Anhembi Morumbi	8675	
23	Universidade Metodista De São Paulo	8350	
24	Universidade Braz Cubas	7947	
25	Universidade Do Tocantins	7831	
26	Universidade Tiradentes	7672	
27	Universidade Federal Fluminense		7442
28	Universidade Salvador	6227	
29	Universidade Estadual Do Maranhão		5509
30	Universidade Federal Da Paraíba		5332
31	Universidade Federal Do Estado Do Rio De Janeiro		5206
32	Centro Universitário Herminio Ometto	5068	
33	Universidade Federal De Sergipe		4707
34	Universidade Do Estado Da Bahia		4634
35	Universidade Federal Rural Do Rio De Janeiro		4387
36	Universidade Potiguar	4271	
37	Universidade Cruzeiro Do Sul	3756	
38	Universidade Estadual De Maringá		3339
39	Universidade Federal Do Ceará		3315

(continued)

Table 1 (continued)

Size	Institutions	Private	Public
40	Universidade Federal De Alagoas		3083
41	Universidade Federal De Ouro Preto		3074
42	Centro Universitário Jorge Amado	2881	
43	Universidade Federal Do Rio De Janeiro		2871
44	Universidade Do Vale Do Rio Dos Sinos	2746	
45	Universidade Estadual Do Ceará		2627
46	Centro Universitário Tupy	2565	
47	Universidade Federal Do Rio Grande Do Norte		2502
48	Universidade Salgado De Oliveira	2485	
49	Universidade Federal De Pelotas		2443
50	Universidade Federal De Juiz De Fora		2374
Total		1,173,399	71,955

Table 2 Undergraduate enrollments in distance education

Institution type	2009	2010	2011	2012	2013	2014
Public	172,394	181,318	177,924	181,624	154,553	139,373
Private	665,037	749,318	815,138	932,334	999,087	1,202,503
Total	837,431	930,636	993,062	1,113,958	1,153,640	1,341,876

Table 3 Degree programs of distance education and campus-based students

Campus-based		Distanced-based	
Bachelor	73.1%	Bachelor	28.8%
Licenciatura[a]	12.4%	Licenciatura[a]	37.4%
Technological[b]	13.6%	Technological[b]	33.9%
Not applicable	0.8%	Not applicable	0.0%

[a]While a Bachelor degree program generally offers a broader intellectual preparation for the teaching profession (as well as many others), the *licenciatura*, or course to prepare individuals for teaching specific subjects of the curriculum in schools, while shorter in content connected to the specific subject, adds on useful components such as educational psychology and pedagogy
[b]Courses grouped together under the title "Technological Courses" usually have nothing whatever to do with technology. Rather, they are post-secondary courses of shorter duration, generally from 2 to 3 years, much like those in community colleges in the United States, and do not qualify the degree-holder for admission into conventional post-graduate programs

The degree-programs chosen by newly-enrolled tertiary students in 2014 was as follows (Table 3).

The manpower question arises here: the majority of new tertiary students choose professions *not* identified as badly needed by Brazilian society; instead of opting for needed, and well-remunerated, specializations in, for example, chemistry and physics

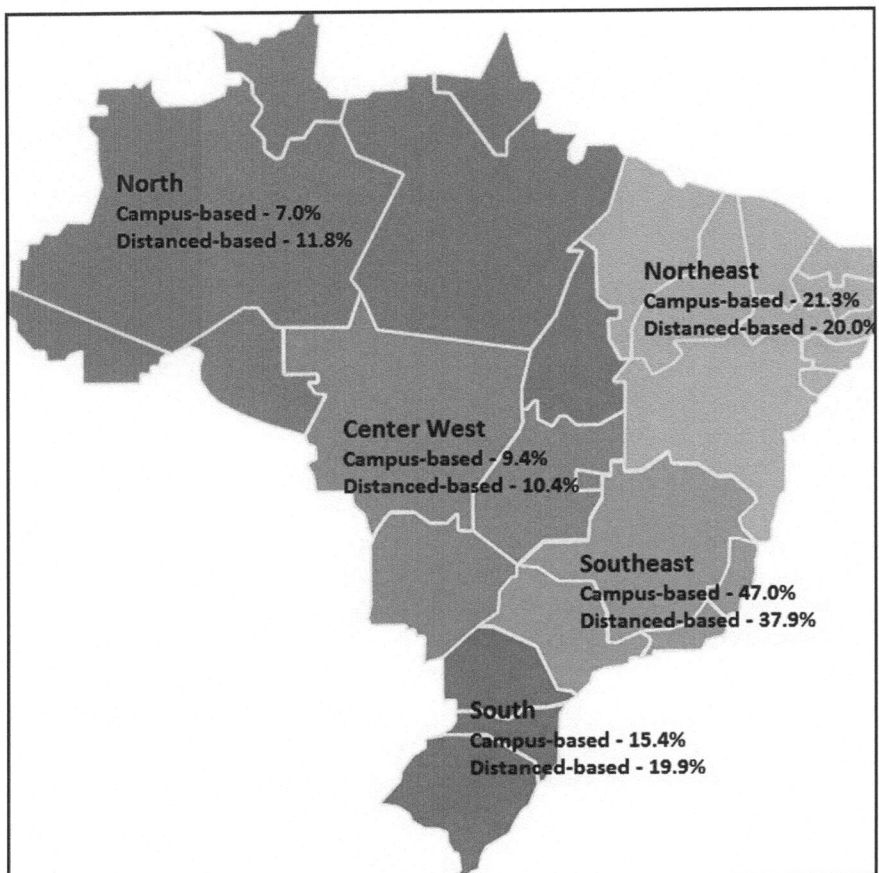

Fig. 1 Regional distribution of tertiary institutions

(only 1.5% of new entrants choose these fields), they opt, instead, for administration and law (which, like medicine, veterinary science and journalism, are undergraduate degrees in Brazil) and pedagogy and *licenciatura* (teaching in schools of language and literature, history, and mathematics). Of those choosing pedagogy and history, 60% choose to study through on-line programs. Many also select social work and nursing, only to later discover that the professional societies in these areas discriminate against those who studied in distance-based programs, even the ones evaluated and approved by the Ministry of Education.

Despite sometimes horrendous working conditions and "undistinguished" remuneration, the profession of school teacher still attracts many new students. The Ministry of Education has approved 4282 different courses in pedagogy and *licenciatura*, 11.9% of which are so new that they have not yet been evaluated; of the 169 programs of this area approved for distance delivery, 10.4% are considered "insufficient," perhaps for lack of an adequate evaluation.

An important consideration in all education is the phenomenon of student dropout, that is, when learners abandon a course or an institution, and the motives and consequences for the student, and for the institution. It is a subject which often comes up when campus-based and distance-based modalities are compared, and generally is provoked by personal or contextual factors related to the student, as well as by elements of the nature or operation of the course. The Syndicate of Chief Executives of Private Institutions of Higher Education of the State of São Paulo (SEMESP) has collected and published relevant and interesting data on evasion, the graphic illustrates comparative results of public and private institutions of the abandoning students (Table 4).

Post-graduate studies that are distance-based normally would be considered less-difficult to operate (because of the greater maturity and autonomy of the learners) and less of a challenge to the vested professional interests in society, but they nevertheless have grown with worrisome slowness. Almost all of the post-graduate programs approved by the Ministry are those giving "professional masters degrees" (such as an MBA, i.e., not requiring the elaboration and public defense of a research-based thesis, and hence having less prestige, especially in the academic world). Following local customs, the Ministry generally waives rigorous supervision of public institutions, and applies sometimes excessive scrutiny to the activities of private institutions. Curiously enough, in the case of distance-based post-graduate studies, it has given high-prestige "*stricto* sensu" status to the above-mentioned distance-based "professional masters degrees" for public school teachers of mathematics, physics, history and literature (UAB 2014) (Table 5).

The best evidence for the general retardation of tertiary distance-based studies in Brazil can be found in the all-important PNE-National Plans for Education, strategic documents orienting formal learning at all levels for ten-year periods, prepared by elements in the Ministry of Education, together with contributions from society in general (such as professors from the faculties of teacher-preparation, syndicates (unions) of teachers and professors, and organizations closely tied to political parties) and, after several public hearings, they are approved, as laws, by the National Congress. The first PNE was issued in 1962, and the most recent one, treating the period 2014–2024, approved only in 2016. Eighty-six pages in length, it mentions distance-based learning only four or five times, and then, only in passing. The document extensively refers to the importance of fulfilling the educational needs of indigenous, isolated and itinerant populations in the country, but never makes the

Table 4 Dropout rates of undergraduate students

Institution type and mode	2012	2013
Private and community institutions—face to face	27.7	27.4
Private institutions—DE	27.4	29.2
Public HEIs—face to face	17.2	17.8
Public HEIs—DE	22.6	25.6

link between them and the possibility of the contribution of distance-based learning. Although 14% of Brazilians have "special needs" (33,377 of them study in tertiary institutions, 13,723 in public ones and 19,664 in private ones) there is no mention of the desirability of connecting this important segment of the population to distance-based studies (MEC/INEP "Sinopse" 2014a).

The Relationship Between Distance Education and More Established and Older Campus-Based, Residential Institutions

There are very few "residential" institutions in Brazil's higher education, notably to be found in universities dedicated to agricultural and veterinary sciences and located in distinctively rural areas, and a handful of small, distinguished specialized institutions, like the Institute of Aeronautical Technology. Almost all tertiary students are gainfully employed when not in class, do not participate in the sparse offerings of on-campus extra-curricular activities, and have no interest in forming or joining alumni associations. In a word, to use a North American term, campus-based students and professors in Brazil are essentially, "streetcar riders," going to and from the campus each day (or only several times a week) for classes, while distance-based learners, required by law to participate in campus-based learning activities, simply are somewhat less-frequent streetcar riders.

Table 5 Academic areas covered by the post-graduate courses

Area	Frequency	Percentage (%)
Agriculture and Veterinary Sciences	29	0.7
Social Science, Administration, Law	1549	39.3
Science, Mathematics, Computation	173	4.4
Education	1307	33.2
Engineering, Construction	110	2.8
Humanities and Arts	250	6.4
Health, Social Welfare	477	12.1
Services (Tourism, Hospitality, Sports, etc.)	41	1.0
Total	3935	100

The Relationship Between the Public and Private Sector Distance Education

There is, in fact, practically no relationship between the two universes, either in campus-based learning or in that which is distanced-based. The private sector is composed of three types of institution: "confessional," which are linked to the major religious sects (Catholicism, Methodism, Presbyterian, Baptist, among others), are not-for-profit, maintain respectable research activities, and enjoy high regard in the community; "community faculties," some of which are, in part, connected to local municipal governments but nevertheless charge tuition fees to students, while others are called "philanthropic" because they are entirely owned by important local families but offer a large number of tuition-waivers to needy students and hence are exempt from taxes, even though they are profit-making—they are not known for having research traditions, but in some cases practice free community-service activities, such as legal and dental support, an extension of their professional courses; and conglomerates of institutions entirely owned by large, profit-seeking, corporate organizations, some with headquarters in other countries—they have highly-professional managers, skillful student-recruiting marketing, take advantage of the opportunities that scalable online distance education can offer, make no attempt at maintaining research activities or contributing to the academic community at large with a university press—one of them is the world's largest educational services corporation based on its student enrollments of over one million.

Future Developments of Distance Education in Brazil

In the short-range future it is expected that campus-based learning will see a significant reduction in student numbers, attributable to the economic recession currently in progress and the prominence of the income-dependent private sector in the offering of undergraduate studies. Distance-based studies, however, will continue to grow because of their greater convenience for working students and their lower tuition costs. Brazilians in general have an extremely high adoption rate of things audio-visual and communicative, which makes possible the prediction that online learning, with its time-shifting possibilities and the increasing use of locally-produced, technology-supported animations, simulations and personal-learning-environment strategies substituting the tedious conventional classroom, has a very bright future. That is, if government bureaucrats and anachronistic academic decision-makers reduce their excessively suspicious treatment of experimentation and creativity in the operation and development of distance-based studies. The 63 million speakers of Portuguese in Europe, Africa and Asia (when added to the 200 million in Brazil) also represent a non-trivial extended market for Brazilian-produced distance-based learning.

The fact that the total number of tertiary students in Brazil represents just under 20% of the country's cohort group of young people, 18–24 years of age, while neighboring countries like Argentina and Chile have over 30% of their young people enrolled in higher education (and North American and European nations enjoy numbers reaching and even exceeding 60%), should be an indicator of needed growth in this sector. Similarly, only 11% of the working-age population of Brazil holds a higher education diploma. But the conservative vision held by many individuals and organizations involved in education, and regarding new approaches to learning in Brazil, is not encouraging. In a recent interview, one official admitted that "there's need for planned expansion, but there's also a risk of advancing in the dark." The scenario of distance-based learning in Brazil is still far from consolidated; the modality is not yet duly institutionalized in the structure of the country's higher education. Nevertheless, many hearts and minds are at work in the task of gaining acceptance for this "solution," so widely-accepted in other countries, to become a major tool to advance Brazil's social and economic development.

Acknowledgements I wish to thank the following colleagues who generously assisted me in organizing the data presented here and made suggestions for improvement of the final draft: Marcia Figueiredo, Luciano Sathler, Renato Bulcão, Marcos Formiga, and Beatriz Roma Marthos.

References

Alves, J. R. M. (2009). A história de EAD no Brasil. In F. M. Litto & M. Formiga (Eds.), *Educação a Distância-o estado da arte* (Vol. 1, pp. 9–13). Pearson and ABED: São Paulo.
Associação Brasileira de Educação a Distância-ABED. (2015). *Analytic report of distance learning in Brazil*. São Paulo: ABED and Uninter. www.abed.org.br/censoead2014/CensoEAD2014_ingles.pdf.
Azevedo, J. C. (2012). Os primórdios da EAD na educação superior brasileira. In F. M. Litto & M. Formiga (Eds.), *Educação a Distância-o estado da arte* (Vol. 2, pp. 2–5). Pearson and ABED: São Paulo.
Conselho Nacional da Educação. (2014). *National policies and norms for the offering of programs and courses of higher education in the distance modality*. http://portal.mec.gov.br/index.php?option=com_docman&view=download&alias=31361-parecer-cne-ces-564-15-pdf&Itemid=30192.
Instituto Nacional De Estudos E Pesquisas. (2012). Diretoria de Estatísticas Educacionais. *Censo de Educação Básica 2012*.
Instituto Nacional De Estudos E Pesquisas Educacionais Anísio Teixeira. (2014a). Censo da educação superior: Sinopse estatística da educação superior 2014. Brasília, DF. http://download.inep.gov.br/informacoes_estatisticas/sinopses_estatisticas/sinopse_educacao_superior/sinopse_educacao_superior_2014.zip.
Instituto Nacional De Estudos E Pesquisas Educacionais Anísio Teixeira. (2014b). Censo da educação superior 2014. Brasília, DF. http://download.inep.gov.br/educacao_superior/censo_superior/documentos/2015/censo_da_educacao_superior_2014_principais_resultados.xls.
Litto, F., Filatro, A., & André, C. (2005). Brazilian research on distance learning, 1999–2003: A state-of-the-art study. *Open Praxis—The Electronic Journal of the International Council for Open & Distance Education*. http://www.abed.org.br/congresso2004/por/pdf/180-TC-D4.pdf.

Litto, F. M. (2011). Escolas Abertas e a Aprendizagem. *Revista FGV Online, 1*(1), 38–49 (Accompanies translation: "Open Schools and Learning"). http://sv.www5.fgv.br/fgvonline/revista/eds/ed1/paginas/pdf/Revista_Completa_ing.pdf.

Moraes, R. B. D. (2013). *Bibliografia Brasiliana* (pp. 239–240). Rio de Janeiro: Livraria Kosmos. http://www.brown.edu/Facilities/John_Carter_Brown_Library/exhibitions/CB/cunha.htm.

Universidade Aberta do Brasil. (2014). Quais são os cursos pós-graduação stricto sensu a distância? www.uab.capes.gov.br/index.php/leis/29-a-UAB-possui-cursos-de-mestrado-ou-doutorado.

Brazil—Commentary

Maria Renata da Cruz Duran and Adnan Qayyum

The Brazilian population of 210 million people are concentrated along the cost, in the northeast, south and southeast regions. In the countryside, we find a population where information, information and communication technologies, and education are harder to access. Yet, from 2000 to 2014 the number of students in higher education rose from 2.6 million to 7.8 million. These numbers were divided between on campus courses (presencialmente) with 83% of enrollments, and open and distance learning (ODL) with 17%. The majority of ODL courses were offered by the private sector. Still, public sector ODL achieved an enrollment growth of 93.9% between 2005 and 2009. This decreased to 19% for the following five years. The rise and fall in public sector ODL enrollments is connected to Open University of Brazil system (Universidade Aberta do Brasil or UAB), whose importance is the subject of this commentary.

The UAB system was created in 2006 to connect public institutions of higher education with state and municipal delegates, and the federal government. Specifically, the goal was to provide higher education for public teachers in regions not served by traditional institutions. The UAB is also responsible for the National Public Administration Training Program, offering undergraduate courses in public administration and specializations in public management and public health. In the strictest sense, UAB is not a conventional higher education institution, nor a ODE institution. Rather it is a system that regulates student entrance and admissions, and copyrights instructional materials. The "open" in the name of UAB comes from the extensive range of students and geography covered, and from the intention of its' creators.

M. R. da Cruz Duran (✉)
Modern and Contemporary History, Universidade Estadual de Londrina, Londrina, Brazil
e-mail: mariarenataduran@gmail.com

A. Qayyum
Lifelong Learning and Adult Education, Pennsylvania State University, State College, PA, USA
e-mail: adnan@psu.edu

The Coordinator for the Improvement of Higher Education (CAPES) is the authority that funds, regulates and manages the courses offered by higher education institutions at in person (presencial) support centers (SPCs). Since 2007, the Coordinator for the Improvement of Higher Education had its budget tripled and responsibilities expanded to include teacher training. This initiative was divided into two directories: Basic Education and Distance Education.

Distance Education directories have had two phases. In the first, from 2005–2011, the UAB system was created according to rules of the National Plan for Teacher Training and the Joint Action Plan for teacher training support. At the time, a collegial system of management was created, including regional and area forums. The management was composed of the first UAB teachers and managers. The second phase was from 2011 to 2016. By that time there were over 170 000 enrollments within the UAB system. There was also a movement to evaluate public higher education institutions, and support centers, leading to a replacement of collegial management with a group of specialists.

The UAB emerged from traditional institutions that already offered the same course from a face-to-face mode to an ODL format. The public Brazilian ODL mode is more like a blended format, where 30% of activities, especially assessments and evaluations take place at support centers. Support centers are a key part of public ODL in Brazil. The support centers are partly based on the system at the Spanish national DE institution, the Universidad Nacional de Educación a Distancia. The physical space of the support center is a mix of popular culture and scientific knowledge for a digital world. Their characteristics follow the dual nature of coast and countryside that is the basis of ODL in Brazil. Small locations, far from the coast, have support centers with more cultural activities, educational materials and interaction with local education groups. Support centers in medium sized towns and cities are a cradle of new or hybrid course materials. These support centers are meeting points where technological tools and resources for general teacher training are available. In big cities, support centers have digital infrastructure and materials. The combination of public institutions of higher education and support centers results in a kaleidoscope system, where social interests and federal policies can combine to foster digital culture and enrich knowledge.

The UAB system budget is oriented to supporting this model. However, the government funding model affects autonomy, as the UAB system is based on grants and benefits not on a permanent budget. At one point recently, the UAB System went for one and a half years without monies as the national budget was not passed on university funding. Many new educational program offerings had to be suspended. Further, the UAB system is limited in being able to expand its programs for possible funding sources. For example, legislation does not allow for payment benefits to foreign citizens. So UAB system initiatives are limited to national programs and is restricted from expanding into Africa among other places. Moreover, UAB was affected by a new public policy that focused on technical training at the high school level. This divided the ODL budget. Instead of seeing an expansion of funding, it was cut by 75% when the Coordinator for the Improvement of Higher Education budget was announced in 2015.

Finally, another challenge for public ODL in Brazil is still infrastructure: internet speed is usually very low in public institutions, when there is connectivity at all. The technology and computer science sectors, as well as many universities and libraries are not yet prepared for digital activities that, outside their walls, grows exponentially. In general, we find ourselves at a time when it is difficult to know whether the public ODL will continue to receive the investment needed for its growth. It should be noted that despite all this, the UAB system has a dropout rate that is ten percent lower than private sector distance education. Public ODL in Brazil is a teaching and delivery mode that can provide quality, flexible educational programs at scale for a knowledge society.

Canada

Tony Bates

Introduction

Canada is the second largest country in the world by total area, yet its population is only 35 million. Even though nearly 80% of the Canadian population live near the southern border with the USA, and in its larger cities, Canada is still in general a sparsely populated country, with long distances between urban centres, and between urban centres and their vast hinterland. There are therefore strong geographical reasons for distance education.

At the same time, Canada's closeness to and strong connections with the USA, its economically advanced cities, and a well-educated work force, have resulted in ideal conditions for the development of advanced digital applications such as online learning. Indeed, we shall see that Canada has been at the leading edge of online and distance education developments.

The Canadian Higher Education System

Education is constitutionally the responsibility of the ten provinces and the three territories. Thus there is no *national* higher education system in Canada. There is no Federal Ministry or Department with responsibility for post-secondary education, although the federal government does provide student aid and tax breaks for students and their parents, and funding for research and innovation. The federal government is largely responsible for funding higher education opportunities for aboriginal learn-

T. Bates (✉)
Ryerson University, Toronto, Canada
e-mail: tony.bates@ubc.ca

© The Author(s) 2018   49
A. Qayyum and O. Zawacki-Richter (eds.), *Open and Distance Education in Australia, Europe and the Americas*, SpringerBriefs in Open and Distance Education,
https://doi.org/10.1007/978-981-13-0298-5_6

ers, although aboriginals who go on to post-secondary education usually attend a provincially funded institution.

There are four types of public post-secondary institution in Canada:

- universities,
- polytechnics/institutes of technology,
- one- and two-year professional and vocational colleges,
- CEGEPs (general and vocational colleges) in Québec.

Almost all universities are provincially funded and there are almost no private, for-profit online universities in Canada. New Brunswick is the exception, with two private, for-profit universities (University of Fredericton and Yorkville University) with provincial legal status, but they are not recognised by Universities Canada, the national organization of universities, and their programs are small. There are numerous private, for-profit vocational colleges, but still a majority of two-year college students attend provincially funded institutions.

Students pay tuition fees that vary considerably from province to province, ranging from $2660 a year in Newfoundland to $7868 in Ontario. The average nationally is C$6191. The fees for provincial two-year colleges are usually much lower. International students however pay full tuition fees that can range between $15,000 and $20,000 a year for undergraduates. Most Canadian students receive financial support of some kind, ranging from endowment-funded scholarships to low interest student loans to tax breaks. In most provinces, grants and tax-breaks combined usually cover at least the tuition costs.

Distance Students

Because there is no federal agency responsible for higher education, there are no official national statistics on the number of students taking online or distance courses. However, a more recent survey (2017) found that online course enrolments for credits constitute about 16% of all university course enrolments, and 12% of all college course enrolments. Online enrolments had increased by 10% per annum in universities and by 15% per annum in colleges outside Québec over the period 2011-2015.

Almost 40% of the Canadian population live in Ontario. A census in 2010 of all its universities conducted by the Ontario Ministry of Training, Colleges and Universities (Ontario 2011) found there were 500,000 online course registrations equal to 25,000 full-time equivalent students (11% of all post-secondary registrations). This survey included colleges as well as universities.

Many universities report that the number of online courses, and student enrolments in fully online courses and programs, has been slowly but steadily increasing for the last 15–20 years, and at a faster rate than on-campus enrolments.

Some provincial governments, such as British Columbia, Alberta and Ontario, have encouraged the growth of online learning by special funding for the development of new online courses in addition to the annual government operating grants for universities and colleges.

Distance Teaching Universities

There are two public universities in Canada that offer programs only at a distance:

- **Athabasca University**, established in 1970, and funded by the Alberta government, is an open, fully distance university that draws up to 40% of its 40,000 students from outside the province of Alberta. It offers both undergraduate and graduate degrees fully at a distance. Its Master in Distance Education started in 1994 and is still running today. It also offers a Doctor of Education in Distance Education, the first of its kind in North America.
- **TÉLUQ** (formerly TeleUniversité) in Québec is a francophone, fully distance university offering full degree programs to just under 20,000 students a year. It is part of the province's multi-campus Université du Québec, which awards the degrees and diplomas.

However, both these institutions are facing existential challenges as more and more conventional universities offer fully online courses and programs.

Thompson Rivers University, a campus-based, provincially funded institution in British Columbia, also offers distance courses and programs through its Open Learning Division (TRU-OL). TRU-OL partners with three other BC universities to ladder their distance education courses towards a TRU degree.

Royal Roads University (RRU), on Vancouver Island in British Columbia, offers a mix of online and on-campus programs, focusing on graduate level career development. RRU offers three formats:

- on-site with 100% face to face learning;
- blended, with part of the program taught in a face to face residency and the balance on line; and
- fully on-line.

RRU's residency based programs are usually short, ranging from one to three weeks, usually in the summer. The majority of its programs are fully online.

Dual-Mode Institutions

Many of the campus-based universities and two-year colleges in Canada also offer distance education courses, usually fully online. Some of the universities have a long history of distance education provision. Queen's University (Ontario) offered its first correspondence courses in 1889 and overcame geographical challenges in regions without access to the postal service by employing the North West Mounted Police (now the Royal Canadian Mounted Police) to deliver material for these courses (CADE 1999).

Since the advent of online learning in the 1990s, many campus-based Canadian universities and some two-year colleges and CEGEPs now offer a wide range of online distance education programs. There are basically four types of distance education courses commonly offered:

- individual fully online courses, serving several purposes:
  - enabling students who have dropped courses, or need only one or two more courses, to complete their undergraduate degrees without having to come back full-time for another year;
  - providing more flexibility in scheduling for students throughout their academic studies;
  - offering increased access for working adults/students with young families;
- courses towards a full undergraduate degree available entirely online;
- post-graduate masters programs, mainly aimed at working professionals;
- non-credit courses or programs leading to certificates or diplomas.

Many of these dual mode universities offer parallel on-campus and distance courses and do not indicate the mode of delivery on degree transcripts. Indeed in most cases on-campus and distance students take the same examination, usually under supervision at a proctored exam site or more recently through online proctoring.

Although the majority of students in Canada are taking just one or two online courses as part of their on-campus program, over the last two years some conventional universities have also started offering complete undergraduate degree programs fully online. For instance, students can start a B.Tech program in computing at Mohawk College then transfer to McMaster University to complete the last two years fully online. Similarly, Queen's University is offering a fully online B.Tech in mining engineering aimed at working miners across Ontario. Fully distance undergraduate programs though are still quite rare in Canada, the main providers still being Athabasca University, TRU-OL and TÉLUQ.

In every province there is at least one campus-based university also offering online and distance education:

- in **British Columbia**, Simon Fraser University has almost 20,000 distance course enrolments per annum, 8% of all enrolments (SFU 2015). The University of British Columbia has just under 90 distance courses for credit and about 9000 distance education course enrolments;
- Athabasca University is the main provider of online and distance education programs in **Alberta** at a university level, but several of the colleges have extensive online courses and programs. Southern Alberta Institute of Technology has a unique program for women in Afghanistan, who take a diploma in business management online from SAIT through the Afghan-Canadian school in Kandahar City. More than 2000 women in Afghanistan have graduated from this program;

- both the University of **Saskatchewan** and the University of **Manitoba** have substantial distance programs;
- in **Ontario**, at least 15 of the 24 universities offer distance education programs. Laurentian University offers over 350 online and distance courses in both the English and French languages. Laurentian is the largest bilingual provider of distance education in Canada. The University of Ottawa also offers online and distance courses and programs both in English and French;
- in **Québec**, Laval University has a very large francophone distance education program. Laval also has a partnership with the African Virtual University, which uses some of Laval's courses in francophone African countries;
- all universities and colleges in **New Brunswick** are currently offering distance education courses using various methods;
- In **Nova Scotia**, which has a large number of small universities, several also offer distance education courses and programs;
- in **Newfoundland** Memorial University has a large online program. In the fall of 2013, 1441 students were distance education only (8%) and 4161 students (22%) took at least one distance education course. There were over 17,000 online course enrolments in total. Their online enrolments have increased by 50% over 10 years (Memorial University of Newfoundland 2014).

Meta-Organizations

Several provinces have established meta-level organizations to help co-ordinate or encourage online learning, although these organizations do not offer online courses or programs themselves.

BCcampus evaluates emerging educational technologies and has also in the past managed a fund from the provincial government to support the development of new online courses and open educational resources, and more recently (2012–2016) has managed funds for developing open textbooks. It has also established an open educational resources repository available worldwide.

Contact North|Contact Nord in Ontario, established in 1986, offers five core services in English and French. The five services include:

- 112 local online learning centres serving 600 small, remote, rural, aboriginal, and francophone communities;
- a portal of online courses and programs from Ontario institutions for students and prospective students;
- a portal for faculty and instructors, focusing on online learning;
- a portal for students needing literacy and basic skills training;
- a Student Information Hotline providing support to students and prospective students.

eCampus Alberta, eCampus Manitoba, eCampus Ontario and **Contact North/Contact Nord** provide online portals for students where all the courses offered by most of the universities and colleges within the province are listed.

The **Council of Ontario Universities** manages a fund from the Ontario Ministry of Training, Colleges and Universities for developing online courses and creating shared open educational resources, through a competitive bidding process.

These organizations also often support faculty development initiatives for online learning, through webinars and local conferences and workshops. They also facilitate professional communities of practice. In British Columbia, for instance, the **Educational Technology Users Group** (ETUG) is supported by BCcampus.

The Canadian Virtual University (**CVU**) is a partnership of 11 Canadian universities collaborating in the development and marketing of distance and online education. The CVU does not offer courses or degrees itself but serves as a portal service for its members. CVU is governed by a board of directors, consisting of presidents and directors of distance education at participating universities. Collectively, the CVU offer over 2500 distance and online courses, and over 350 complete degrees, diplomas, and certificates. One quarter of CVU's programs and courses are offered in French. In Canada, there can be barriers in transferring credit or qualifications between institutions. Difficulties with inter-institutional credit transfer are a limiting factor for institutions wishing to develop national online or distance programs. However, CVU universities accept each other's courses for transfer credit, thus providing students with greater course selection than is available at any single university.

Several Canadian institutions (Athabasca, TRU-OL, Kwantlen Polytechnic, Portage College, BCcampus, eCampus Alberta and Contact North) are members of **OERuniversitas (OERu)**, which offers free online courses so that learners can gain formal credentials from the partner institutions. OERu is a consortium of 36 organizations across five continents, and is dedicated to widening access and reducing the cost of post-secondary education by providing open pathways to formal, quality credentials.

The **Commonwealth of Learning**, charged with promoting open distance education throughout the 53 countries of the Commonwealth, is located in Vancouver, British Columbia.

There are several Canada-wide organizations that support online and distance educators, including:

- the Canadian Network for Innovation in Education (**CNIE**), created in 2007 through the amalgamation of the Canadian Association of Distance Education (CADE) and the Association for Media and Technology in Education in Canada (AMTEC);
- the Canadian Association for University Continuing Education (**CAUCE**);
- Canada's Collaboration for Online Higher Education Research (**COHERE**);
- **REFAD** (Network for Francophone Distance Education in Canada) supports francophone distance educators.

Quality Assurance and Quality Control

Most provinces have degree quality assurance boards for provincially funded universities and colleges, and an accreditation board for private colleges. However, well-established provincial universities in particular have a great deal of autonomy, using standard procedures to approve courses and programs through academic departments and Senate. This applies equally to online and distance courses, which in general follow the same procedures, but often with more internal scrutiny.

Funding models and practices vary considerably for distance education programs in Canada. Most institutions require a faculty member to be responsible for online courses leading to credit, although that faculty member may not teach all sections of the course. Thus there are likely to be some part-time sessional or adjunct instructors involved in the delivery, especially where the class size is large. Through the use of sessional instructors as well as full-time faculty, instructor: student ratios are at a level where there is regular and ongoing interaction between students and an instructor.

One of the main factors ensuring quality control in Canadian online learning is the use of a team approach for course development, usually involving a full-time faculty member working with an instructional designer, who in turn can call on specialist media designers. Also instructional designers ensure that courses are using Universal Design principles to create inclusive learning environments, and that the most appropriate pedagogy for distance learning is used. Some, such as the University of British Columbia, use a formal quality assurance tool for its online courses.

Most online courses for credit in Canadian universities have been built around learning management systems, which provide a platform for content, a structure for student work, tools for asynchronous online, text-based discussion, and ways for students to submit assignments for assessment. More recently there has been growing use of web conferencing and/or recorded video (moving back to a more lecturing approach), or alternatively a greater use of social media such as blogs and wikis, and e-portfolios for assessment that encourage student content creation and communication (moving to a more learner-controlled or learner-centred approach). Thus the relative homogeneity of course design that typified Canadian online learning since 1995 is now beginning to splinter, although the LMS-based course is still dominant.

Although there are no national figures, most Canadian universities and colleges report online completion rates within 5–10% of students taking the same course via campus classes. For instance the Ontario 2010 survey found that completion rates for individual online courses were an average of 89% for universities and 79% for colleges.

However, as for face-to-face teaching, quality can vary from institution to institution and from course to course. In general though, quality in online teaching is not seen as a major issue in most provincially funded institutions in Canada.

Innovation and Research

Canada has a long and substantial record of innovation and research in open and online education.

Innovation in Open Education

Athabasca University was founded in 1970 by the Alberta government. Its design model, based on open access, print-based courses, continuous enrolment, individual tutors and self-paced independent learning was markedly different from the U.K. Open University's, which also started at roughly the same time. Athabasca also began offering the first fully online degree programs in 1994, including the first fully online MBA in the world.

British Columbia became the first jurisdiction in North America to implement open textbooks. At the end of 2015 there were 136 open textbooks in the BCcampus project, adapted or created by BC faculty, for all 'core' subjects at university and college level. All these books are available for free downloading under a Creative Commons license, and are offered in various e-book formats free of charge, or as print on demand books available at the cost of printing. As of 25 February, 2016, the project has resulted in estimated savings for students of between $1.2 and $1.4 million. BC also recently partnered with Alberta, Saskatchewan and Campus Manitoba to assist them in their own roll out of open textbooks. Algonquin College in Ontario has also launched an e-textbook initiative, working with the publishing industry to provide e-books for all courses.

The province of Alberta has implemented a $2 million initiative to promote and support the use of Open Educational Resources in higher education institutions in Alberta. The province is collaborating with British Columbia and Saskatchewan on a common OER repository.

Innovation in Online Learning

Canada has been a pioneer in online learning. CoSy was an early computer conferencing system developed by the University of Guelph in Ontario in 1983, and was later used by the U.K. Open University for its first courses using online teaching in 1988.

The first fully online course for university credit was offered in 1986 at the Ontario Institute of Studies in Education, a graduate school of the University of Toronto. This was a course for 20 for-credit and 20 non-credit students designed and delivered by Professor Linda Harasim and her colleague, Dorothy Smith. The course was on 'Women and Computers', using 150 or 300 baud modems via the public telephone network. TÉLUQ (then called Télé-université) also used CoSy for computer conferencing as early as 1989.

TeleEducation New Brunswick developed a DOS-based learning management system in eastern Canada in 1994 and also the TeleCampus, incorporating a distance education website and a metadata depository of online courses.

The first web-based learning management system, WebCT, was developed at the University of British Columbia in 1996 by Murray Goldberg, and acquired in 2006 by Blackboard, Inc. WebCT was being used by 10 million students in 80 countries at that time. In 2000, the University of Guelph partnered with Desire2Learn, a Canadian company based in Kitchener, Ontario, to develop another major learning management system, now called Brightspace.

The University of British Columbia began offering fully online courses for credit in 1995, and also offered its first fully online programs in 2003, a Master in Educational Technology, developed in collaboration with Tec de Monterrey in Mexico (offered both in English and Spanish), and a Master in Adult Education and Global Learning, in cooperation with three international partner universities. UBC is also one of five partner universities in an Asia-Pacific collaboration to create an online certificate program in sustainable forestry management. All these programs are still running 13 years later.

Another important development is the move to full cost-recovery graduate online programs aimed at career development. These use a business model that covers all costs, including university overheads, from 'standard' tuition fees. These business models may need up to seven years before costs are fully recovered, but the business model allows new research faculty to be hired from the increased revenues, as these are new students, often from out of province. Online MBAs, offered by a number of Canadian universities, is another example, but other examples can be found in health, education, creative writing, and engineering.

Dave Cormier, an instructor at the University of Prince Edward Island, was the first to coin the term MOOC (Massive Open Online Course). The first MOOC, *Connectivism and Connective Knowledge* (*CK08*), was offered in 1998 by the Extension Division of the University of Manitoba. This course, designed by George Siemens, Stephen Downes and Dave Cormier, enrolled 27 on-campus students who paid a tuition fee, but it was also offered online for free and attracted a further 2200 students. Downes classified this course and others like it that followed as connectivist or cMOOCs, because of their design, which focused mainly on learners sharing experiences and inter-changing ideas through a range of social media linked by hashtags. However, a majority of MOOCs follow a different design, using mainly video-recorded lectures, based on a model developed in 2011 at Stanford University and MIT in the USA. At the time of writing, eight Canadian universities are offering about 20 MOOCs using a variety of platforms.

Canadian institutions have also been heavily involved in developing resources, courses and programs using mobile learning, virtual worlds, and simulations. For instance,

- the Justice Institute of British Columbia, which trains public safety workers (police, fire services, etc.) offers all of its online learning on mobile platforms (phones, tablets), and uses an in-house designed simulation for training emergency responders;
- Loyalist College in Ontario uses a specially designed virtual border post and a virtual car in teaching Canadian Border Service Agents;
- Ryerson University uses 'virtual' law firms for its online Law Practice Program;
- UBC has developed open access virtual soil science learning resources (Soil-web.ca).

Research in Online and Distance Education

Canada is home to two of the major peer-reviewed academic journals in distance education:

- the *International Journal of E-learning and Distance Education* (formerly the *Journal of Distance Education*, established in 1986).
- the *International Review of Research in Open and Distance Learning* (IRRODL), established in 2000.

Both these are open access and published at Athabasca University by AU Press, Canada's first open access publisher.

The Canadian Initiative for Distance Education Research (CIDER) is a research initiative of IRRODL and Athabasca University's Centre for Distance Education. CIDER sponsors a variety of professional development activities designed to increase the quantity and quality of distance education research, and owes its existence to the drive and leadership of Professor Terry Anderson. Anderson and Randy Garrison of the University of Calgary have been responsible for much of the research and literature on communities of inquiry (Garrison et al. 2000).

There have been two large, research projects in Canada related to online learning, both funded by the federal government. The first was the TeleLearning-NCE project, which was funded to the tune of $13 million for seven years from 1995 to 2002. In some ways this funding was too early as online learning was just developing in this period, and although the project led to the publication of a large number of academic research papers, its impact on practice overall was negligible.

More recent is the Learning and Performance Support Systems (LPSS) program, a $19 million initiative from Canada's National Research Council (2013–2017). The objective of the LPSS is "to build a system where individuals can access, and get credit for, learning from any education provider at all, whether from home, the workplace, or at a school." The lead investigator is Stephen Downes.

In the early 2000s, several universities collaborated in the eduSource project, a collaborative venture among Canadian public and private sector partners to create the prototype for a working network of interoperable learning object repositories using Canada's broadband Internet network CA*Net 4.

However, to date most research into online or distance education in Canada has been conducted either by graduate students as part of dissertations or theses or by individual faculty and/or instructional designers working in relative isolation.

Main Challenges and Future Opportunities

In general online and distance education is increasingly accepted and continues to expand in most Canadian post-secondary institutions, but nevertheless there are a number of challenges that need to be addressed.

The Institutional Organization of Online and Distance Education

Traditionally, dual-mode institutions have located the responsibility for the design and delivery of distance education courses within the university or college's extension or continuing education department. The distance education unit will often manage funds to pay for not only release time for academic staff to design and develop distance courses, but also for the cost of additional sessionals or adjunct faculty to teach the courses. The distance education courses, while as often for credit as non-credit, have traditionally been therefore an 'extra', outside the main work of an academic department, and to a large extent funded from the tuition revenues from the distance education students, with perhaps some revenue sharing with the academic departments.

However, in the last few years there has also been a big shift to hybrid learning, a mix of face-to-face and online learning, on campus. This is a fast evolving area, with a number of different design models. Some universities, such as the University of British Columbia and the University of Ottawa, have formal strategic plans to increase the number of hybrid or flexible learning courses. Both Queen's and Guelph have or are developing university-wide visions and strategies for online and distance education.

As more and more on-campus faculty start to use online components in their class-room teaching, so the demand grows for more technical support, such as instructional and web designers. However, such expertise has traditionally been located outside the main faculty departments, in Continuing Education or Extension.

As a result, a few universities have set up a separate unit, or specialist staff have been hired, to support on-campus e-learning, leaving Continuing Education to man-age the fully distance online courses. However, some deans and academic heads of department have begun to see online learning as a source of new students, and new academic programs, especially at graduate level, and have wanted access to the resources located in Continuing Education, especially if most of the distance education students are taking credit courses as part of their degree.

As a result, some Canadian universities have changed both the organizational and funding model, integrating for-credit online courses and programs within the main academic departments, making faculties responsible for the design, development and delivery of online courses, even if supported by and sometimes dependent on specialist staff. Indeed a number have gone so far as to integrate faculty development, support for the use of on-campus learning technologies, and distance education all into one Centre for Teaching, Learning and Technology. Sometimes large faculties with significant online learning activities may also have their own learning technology support departments.

With educational technology support reporting to the Provost's Office (sometimes through a Vice Provost for Teaching and Learning) or to the Dean of a Faculty, academic departments are then more able to decide for themselves on the best mix of courses and programs. However, such organizational changes can be very disruptive and time consuming.

Better Faculty Development

Rapid developments in learning technologies, the need for teaching methods that help students develop the knowledge and skills needed in a digital society, the increased diversity of the student body, and the increasing integration of online and face-to-face teaching require faculty to have a much higher level of teaching skills, and in particular an understanding of pedagogy and alternative course design models.

Most faculty and instructors in Canada are totally unprepared for such developments. Their training is primarily in research and as subject experts. To date, faculty and instructors have been dependent on substantial help from instructional designers in particular, but adding more support staff as the use of online learning grows takes funding away from academic departments and impacts therefore on instructor: student ratios.

The current system of faculty development in Canada is primarily voluntary. More systematic pre-service as well as in-service programs for faculty development are essential, if the quality of online and distance education is to be maintained as it expands into the mainstream.

New Learner-Centred Pedagogical Models

Perhaps the most interesting development though in Canadian online learning and distance education is in the design of courses that require students to develop the skills of knowledge management (Bates 2015). Instead of an instructor choosing, organizing and delivering academic content, courses are designed so that students collaboratively use the Internet to find, analyse, evaluate and apply knowledge to solve real world problems. E-portfolios are used to demonstrate the knowledge they have acquired. Thus instructors become facilitators and guides rather than deliverers of information. This approach better prepares students for the volatile, uncertain, complex, ambiguous and constantly changing world that they will face on graduating.

Conclusion

Online and distance education continues to grow, and more importantly, online learning has reached a level of acceptance in Canada where it is now being mainstreamed into campus teaching as well as distance education. This is breaking down the previously sharp distinction between face-to-face teaching and distance education.

Many of the conventional universities have moved rapidly into online learning, both for fully distance courses or programs and as part of blended or hybrid learning. This is opening new opportunities, such as fully online professional masters programs that not only bring in new students, often across provincial borders or even internationally, but also brings in new sources of funding, enabling more research faculty to be hired. Above all, online and distance learning offers students in Canada an increasingly wide variety of ways to access post-secondary education.

Acknowledgements Although I take full responsibility for any errors or omissions in the text, I am indebted to the following people who reviewed earlier drafts of this chapter and provided suggestions for the chapter:
Chris Crowley, University of British Columbia
Natalie Giesbrecht, University of Guelph
France Henri, Téluq
Maxim Jean-Louis, Contact North
Rory McGreal, Athabasca University
Gordon Tarzwell, Thompson Rivers University and the Canadian Virtual University

References

Bates, A. (2015). *Teaching in a digital age.* Victoria BC: BCcampus.
Bates, T., Desbiens, B., Donovan, T., Martel, E., Mayer, D., Paul, R., Poulin, R., & Seaman, J. (2017). *Tracking online and distance education in Canadian Universities and Colleges: 2017.* The National Survey of Online and Distance Education in Canadian Post-Secondary Education. Vancouver, Canada.
Canadian Association of Distance Education. (1999). *Open learning and distance education in Canada.* Ottawa: Minister of Public Works and Government Services Canada.
Garrison, R., Anderson, A., & Archer, W. (2000). Critical inquiry in a text-based environment: Computer conferencing in higher education. *The Internet and Higher Education, 2*(3), 87–105.
Memorial University of Newfoundland. (2014). *Enrolment plan 2020.* St. John's NF: Office of the Provost and Vice President (Academic).

Ontario. (2011). *Fact sheet summary of Ontario eLearning surveys of publicly assisted PSE institutions.* Toronto: Ministry of Training, Colleges and Universities.

Simon Fraser University. (2015). *Centre for online distance education statistics.* Burnaby BC: SFU Institutional Research and Planning.

Canada—Commentary

Terry Anderson

Tony Bates, Canada's pre-eminent distance education expert formally retired over 20 years ago—but he forgot to tell those who have relied on his insights and publishing ever since. Thus, Tony is the most qualified Canadian to overview the past but more importantly to forecast the emerging needs and opportunities for distance education institutions, students and researchers in Canada and abroad.

As a typical Canadian, Tony begins by noting the large size of Canada and the sparse population. He correctly notes however that Canada is highly urban with over 75% of Canadians living within 160 km of the United States Border. Thus, Canada has had a need for and a tradition of using distance education to serve rural and isolated learners. However, as in other countries the vast majority of distance learners live and work in urban centres with relatively easy access to campus based institutions. The distance in Canadian online education is more is about time shifting, access, multi-tasking and flexibility than large, empty Canadian landscapes.

Tony next provides the usual lament that, unique in the world, Canada has no national secondary or postsecondary education system—no national targets or plans, no national curriculum, no national education ministry. This anomaly was developed and engraved in our constitutional documents from the intense rivalry and ethnic and cultural distrust amongst Canada's founding populations. However, despite the lack of national coordination that results, the separate provincial systems allows for a great deal of innovation and local adaptation.

I was pleased to see the discussion about the diversity of delivery platforms now emerging with the once predominance of the single institutional LMS being gradually replaced or enhanced by more teacher controlled video courses at one end and aggregated student social media at the other. I can't resist noting Jon Dron's and my development and support over 7 years of a "boutique" social network (Athabasca

T. Anderson (✉)
Emeritus of Distance Education, Athabasca University, Athabasca, AB, Canada
e-mail: terrya@athabascau.ca

© The Author(s) 2018
A. Qayyum and O. Zawacki-Richter (eds.), *Open and Distance Education in Australia, Europe and the Americas*, SpringerBriefs in Open and Distance Education, https://doi.org/10.1007/978-981-13-0298-5_7

Landing) that provides the security and lack of advertisements of a social platform with the student control, wide distribution and archiving of an open network.

To update the description of Canadian MOOCs, a check (February 2017) shows 57 Canadian MOOCs offered by postsecondary institutions. As Tony notes, the largest and most prestigious Universities have partnered with large American MOOC providers—notably Coursera and EdX, while the smaller—medium sized universities are exploring more self-produced options from Canvas or through their own LMS or social network systems.

Tony correctly details the continuing development in Western Canada of open textbooks for both campus and distance delivery. However, there are three other significant Canadian open access initiatives worthy of mention. The world's largest open access research publication system, Open Journal Systems (OJS) was developed by Simon Fraser University and the University of British Columbia. Over 9000 journals are published using the OJS system (including most of the open access distance education DE journals globally) and it now provides hosting, analytics and professional development support. Second, is the number of Canadian founding and current members or OERu, an international organization dedicated to providing free credit courses through collaborative development and support. Finally, Athabasca University Library supports the OER Knowledge Cloud which offers a global database of research articles published on OER development and use.

The chapter ends with the universal and most certainly Canadian challenge of helping faculty to adapt to the quickly changing context of networked living and learning. Of course the necessary personal and institutional changes and new investments come at a time when both private attention and public funding has many competing demands. The old saying that change only happens here through death or retirement will certainly not do! However, if others keep learning and contributing in retirement as Tony has done, the future for Canadian distance education looks promising!

Germany

Ulrich Bernath and Joachim Stöter

Introduction

In reviewing the history and current state of online distance education in Germany, two separate developments are noticeable. Firstly, private initiatives can be traced back to the 1850s, ranging from correspondence to traditional distance and modern online distance education endeavors. In contrast, developments in the public educational sector are more recent, dating back to the 1950s after the Second World War, when Germany was divided in East and West Germany, and later from 1990, when the country was reunified. Distance education in East Germany was fundamentally different from developments in West Germany. East German structures were controlled centrally by the State, whereas in the Federal Republic of West Germany, eleven *Bundesländer* (states) decided autonomously on educational policies, thus resulting in multiple developments.

In 1990, after the reunification of Germany, the Eastern regime and structures collapsed and the West German federal constitution was extended to 16 states. The current picture of online distance education in Germany is a result of 16 autonomous educational policies, supported by a great variety of national funding programs.

Private for-profit institutions, the FernUniversität of Hagen and various specialized online and distance education initiatives at conventional universities share about one third of the total number of distance learners. The FernUniversität of Hagen is state funded and offers tuition-free degree granting programs.

U. Bernath (✉)
Ulrich Bernath Foundation for Research in Open and Distance Learning, Oldenburg, Germany
e-mail: ulrich.bernath@frodl.org

J. Stöter
Carl Von Ossietzky University of Oldenburg, Oldenburg, Germany
e-mail: j.stoeter@uni-oldenburg.de

© The Author(s) 2018
A. Qayyum and O. Zawacki-Richter (eds.), *Open and Distance Education in Australia, Europe and the Americas*, SpringerBriefs in Open and Distance Education,
https://doi.org/10.1007/978-981-13-0298-5_8

In conventional universities, open, online and distance learning initiatives are offered predominantly in life-long continuing and professional education programs that are partly self-supporting. The most acquainted examples are mentioned and discussed in this chapter. Most initiatives in public higher education are originated as state-funded trial runs, and only a few have resulted in sustained and effective practices.

Private Initiatives in Education and Training at a Distance

In Germany, "the evolution of the character and practice of distance education" (Holmberg 1995) is deeply rooted. Usually, records of the history of German distance education refer to Charles Toussaint and Gustav Langenscheidt, the founders of a language school in Berlin in 1856 that offered self-explanatory study letters for language teaching distributed by postal mail. Since their *Methode Toussaint-Langenscheidt* aimed at one-way instruction, it has been debated as to whether they can be viewed as the pioneers of correspondence education in Germany (Delling 1978, pp. 11f.; Holmberg 1995, p. 108, 2005 p. 14). There is less doubt about the so-called *System Karnack-Hachfeld* introduced in 1896 by the publishing house Bonneß & Hachfeld in Potsdam, Germany, supported soon thereafter by a technical school, the *Technikum Frankenhausen am Kyffhäuser*. The study letters developed by this school covered the fields of mechanical and civil engineering comprehensively, and the initiative became a long-lasting success. In this context, the term *Fernunterricht* was coined. *Fern* refers to distance, and *Unterricht* stands for instruction. The Technikum's concept of *Fernunterricht*, originated in 1896 (Delling 1978, pp. 14f.), combined three elements: (i) written study materials (study letters); (ii) written assignments; (iii) two-way correspondence. These methods indicate a pioneering correspondence school, which spawned generations of followers in both the private and public sectors.

Today, in 2016, about 80 private institutions are members of the professional association in Germany, the *Forum DistancE-Learning*,[1] which counts more than 400,000 learners in a wide range of offerings in distance education and training, comprising short courses as well as university-level degree programs.[2] The modern concept of distance education augments the original ideas of correspondence education (dating back to 1896) and includes multiple media for delivering taught programs, e-learning tools, online teaching and learning environments and an emphasis on tutorial support. Such support may be decentralized and face-to-face in regional study centers, or in online discussion fora.

The most ambitious private institution in the field of professional training is the *DAA-Technikum*.[3] Notable in the field of degree-granting higher and continu-

---

[1] http://www.forum-distance-learning.de/ [08.09.2016].
[2] http://www.forum-distance-learning.de/news/5734 [08.09.2016].
[3] www.daa-technikum.de [08.09.2016].

ing distance education providers are subsidiaries of the family-owned *Klett Group*,[4] such as the *Deutsche Weiterbildungsgesellschaft mbH (DWG)*, the *Wilhelm Büchner Hochschule*, the *Europäische Fernhochschule Hamburg (EURO-FH)*, and the *Studiengemeinschaft Darmstadt (SGD)*. The *Klett Group* represents the majority of the current 112 courses of study offered by a total of 16 private institutions.[5]

When tracking the development of *Fernunterricht* in Germany from its beginnings to this day, it becomes apparent that the private sector has established and developed a rather coherent concept of teaching and learning at a distance (Dieckmann and Zinn 2016), characterized by two-way correspondence, including various forms of "mediated student-tutor interaction as a constituent element" (Holmberg 1995, p. 47).

Public Initiatives in Education and Training at a Distance

The provision of teaching and learning at a distance in the public sector in Germany is less clear and is a more recent development than in the case of private providers. The most striking circumstance which had an impact on this field is the division of Germany into East Germany [*Deutsche Demokratische Republik (DDR)*—the German Democratic Republic (GDR)], and West Germany [*Bundesrepublik Deutschland (BRD)*—the Federal Republic of Germany (FRG)]. This was the case during the period 1949–1990, which was then followed by the reunification of Germany.

Public Initiatives in East Germany (1949–1990)

In East Germany *(DDR/GDR)* education was under central state control, which allowed the development of a nation-wide distance teaching system in the early 1950s. This involved almost all institutions of higher education, resulting in an astonishing 25% of all university degrees being granted through this particular mode of *DDR* distance education (Möhle 1986). Initiated as a talent hotbed for recruiting socialist leadership and cadres in the early years of the *DDR*, the system was also needed later to thwart the brain drain when millions of people fled into the West. Adults were attracted by ample leave allowances which allowed them to attend weekend classes at conventional universities. They were offered standard university lectures in addition to printed study material for independent home study. The so-called *Konsultationszenter* (decentralized consultations center) provided advice and support. This massive intervention in the *DDR* university system slowed down in the 1970s when professional development opportunities came to the fore through specialized institutions for higher education and training (Adler 1990; Möhle 1990).

---

[4]https://www.klett-gruppe.de/home/our+business+units/adult+and+continued+education.772.htm [08.09.2016].

[5]http://www.hochschulkompass.de [08.09.2016].

The centrally defined need for qualifications and professional development controlled privileges for attending distance education offerings. The combination of work and study continued to be a driver for developments in distance education in the DDR. However, all these practices came to an almost abrupt end after the unification of Germany in 1990, leaving an unfortunate aftertaste that has burdened the understanding of distance education ever since. This negative impression views distance education as mass education with limited academic freedom, expository teaching and drill, pre-fabricated study materials and poor student support.

Public Initiatives in West Germany (1949–1990) and in Reunified Germany (1990-to Date)

West Germany (*BRD/FRG*) contained eleven Länder (states) until 1990 that were autonomously responsible for their respective educational systems. With the reunification of Germany, the number of educationally autonomous states grew to 16. Today education remains a federal state authority. The first remarkable developments towards teaching and learning at a distance were the *Funkkolleg* (literally translated: radio course of lectures) in 1966 and almost in parallel, the establishment of the *Deutsches Institut für Fernstudien (DIFF)* (the German Institute for Distance Studies) in 1967. Each of these initiatives is now discussed in more detail followed by a section on the *FernUniversität* which was established in 1975.

Funkkolleg

The *Funkkolleg* was set up by the state of *Hessen,* the *Johann Wolfgang Goethe-Universität Frankfurt,* and the *Hessische Rundfunk* (the public radio station of Hesse). The *Funkkolleg* followed the tradition of university extension programs, although applied in an unusual way. Lectures were broadcast on the radio and accompanied by study material for independent learning and local tutor-led discussion circles. These courses reached out to hundreds of thousands of participants, many of whom completed the courses and gained a certificate of more or less the same value as those offered by 'massive open online courses' (MOOCs) today. The *Funkkolleg* could be viewed as a 'massive open radio course', which shows that today's MOOCs are not nearly as innovative as their originators might like to think. In fact, the *Funkkolleg* provided a fairly effective multi-media, mixed mode approach to distance education, which in today's preferred terminology could be considered as 'blended learning'. Most importantly, the *Funkkolleg* has exhibited impressive sustainability and adaptability, as it has continued to exist for over 50 years (Greven 1998). Recent innovations include podcasts and an online platform which was introduced in 2006. A *Kinder-Funkkolleg* was launched in 2011.[6]

---

[6]http://www.ard.de/home/intern/fakten/abc-der-ard/Kinderfunkkolleg/1144824/index.html [09.08.2016].

Deutsches Institut für Fernstudien (DIFF), Hochschulvereinigung für das Fernstudium im Medienverbund (HVF), and FiM-Versuch

In 1967, soon after the establishment of the *Funkkolleg*, the *Deutsches Institut für Fernstudien (DIFF)* at the *University of Tübingen* in the state of *Baden-Württemberg* became another important milestone for the development of distance education in Germany. The mission of the *DIFF* was the development of *Fernstudienlehrgängen* (distance studies teaching materials) for the further education and professional development of teachers (Deutsches Institut für Fernstudien an der Universität Tübingen 1981). This included undergraduate and higher continuing education, as well as the development of study materials to accompany the *Funkkolleg*.

Regarding the Anglo-American discussion about the origin of the term 'distance education' (Moore and Kearsley 1996, p. 198), it is worth noting that the term *Fernstudium* (distance education) and *Hochschulfernstudium* (distance education in higher education) appeared for the first time in the German literature in 1967 (Peters 1967) and then in the title of the first volume of the *DIFF* book series (Dohmen 1968).[7]

From 1967 until its closure in 2001 the *DIFF* was a hub for the development of course materials—it was a highly regarded center of distance education research and a catalyst for bringing together many diverse stakeholders. These included the German states with their keenly protected autonomy in educational policies, and German professors with their untouchable right to decide on what was taught, based on the constitutional Freedom in Research and Teaching Act. Nevertheless, in the late 1960s there was a largely accepted need for the expansion of educational opportunities through new ways and means.

Under such circumstances, three developments are noteworthy:

(a) The *DIFF* established a remarkable research record on various topics, e.g. learning through the medium of text (Mandl et al. 1984), and many other related works. When the *DIFF* was closed in 2001, its research capacities migrated partially into the *Leibniz-Institut für Wissensmedien*—the Knowledge Media Research Center—at the *University of Tübingen*.[8]

(b) The extent of course materials developed under the auspices of the DIFF was impressive and voluminous.[9]

(c) Although the *DIFF* was generously funded and developed instructionally well-designed, research-informed distance education course materials, it was not able to initiate or participate in sustained higher distance education settings. At best, its operating level was continuing education and professional development, hence the non-degree status of its reach into the areas of education and training.

---

[7]http://terrya.edublogs.org/2013/11/25/the-man-who-invented-distance-education/ [09.08.2016].

[8]https://www.iwm-tuebingen.de/www/en/mitarbeiter/ma.html?uid=fhesse [30.07.2016].

[9]The list of all *Studienbriefe* (study letters) created until 1981 can be found at: www.edudoc.ch/static/infopartner/periodika_fs/bis_1997/010280.pdf [07.09.2016].

The FernUniversität and distance education at conventional universities

In the complex situation in Germany in the 1970s, the largest state, *North Rhine-Westphalia*, took distance education initiatives to the greatest possible extent by establishing a distance university, the *FernUniversität*[10] in Hagen, which started operations in autumn 1975. Originally conceptualized by the social democratic government as a bold approach to widen access to higher education (as with the Open University UK), the *FernUniversität* came to reflect the "different social, cultural and academic traditions" in Germany (Peters 2001, p. 200). According to the basic understanding of a (West-) German university the *FernUniversität* was constituted as a research university with the unique distinction of offering single-mode distance teaching.

Entrance requirements for enrollment in general German higher education institutions were applied, with only limited features of an open university as practiced notably by the Open University UK (Zawacki-Richter et al. 2015). *Studienbriefe* (study letters) were written following the highest possible subject-matter related standards and degrees were granted after a selective examination process culminating in face-to-face seminars. Places at these seminars were limited up to around 25 seats, constrained by the teaching load of each individual professor. Thus there was a mix of modes—distance teaching and independent learning in the beginning of a course and face-to-face seminars in the final stages of study. This implied two things: A guarantee of an indisputable and comparable academic degree, but at the same time an inherent conflict between large-scale enrollments and limited output as a consequence of compulsory face-to-face seminars with limited capacity.

Enrollments at the *FernUniversität* grew fast, surpassing 20,000 after four years, and reaching over 80,000 in 2010. In the light of such large numbers, relatively low numbers of completed degrees can be reported. This discrepancy is often explained as a typical drop-out phenomenon of distance education systems (Moore and Kearsley 1996, p. 159 ff.). However, the particular case of the *FernUniversität* must be interpreted in the context not only of limited opportunities to attend the required face-to-face seminars, but also of the academic tradition of a German university, where the so-called drop-out is seen as a result of a robust selection process in order to maintain academic quality. In addition, the *FernUniversität* caters for a different and diverse student body, most of whom are working adults, who welcome the opportunity to have a second chance at higher education, studying part-time. Not all of them are necessarily interested in obtaining a degree, but rather in continuing their education by independently making best use of the print-based course materials provided (Peters 1992).

With the establishment of the *FernUniversität*, distance education took on a new dimension in Germany. The *FernUniversität* attracted students from all West German states and also from abroad; however, local student support was provided only within the state of *North-Rhine Westphalia*. The other states in Germany faced strong pressure to also provide support for their students enrolled at the *FernUniversität*.

---

[10]https://www.fernuni-hagen.de/english/ [09.08.2016].

A novel solution was soon found by seven states which established central units for distance education at ten conventional universities, with the twofold responsibility of (i) supporting students of the *FernUniversität*; and (ii) developing their own distance education programs (Groten 1992; Bernath 1994, 1996; Kappel et al. 2002).

The concept of local student support in study centers of the *FernUniversität* is rather unique. Whereas the British understanding of student support "means that for each course the student has a tutor, whose task is to mark and comment thoroughly on their assignments and to hold optional local tutorial sessions every few weeks" (Daniel 2016, no page ref), the *FernUniversität* accredits a *mentor* for student support. The mentor must be an expert in interpreting the respective subject matter area independently from the professors at the *FernUniversität*, who have exclusive control over assessments and examinations. Thus there is a strict division of labor between the professors who carry the credentials and are responsible for teaching and assessment and the mentors in study centers who are expert partners to the students in supporting their distance learning experience (Bernath 1992).

The Digital Era and New Developments in Teaching and Learning at a Distance

The digital era, which emerged in Germany in the late 90s, had a self-propelling impact on new information and communication technology (ICT)-enhanced teaching and learning as a result of widespread investment in e-learning infrastructure. The whole higher education system was captured by a consistent process of transition towards the application of e-learning tools, preferably as an add-on to the campus-based teaching and learning environment. Solutions at conventional universities became labelled as 'lifelong', 'online', 'blended', 'e-learning' or 'virtual learning'. An example is the state-wide approach adopted by the *Virtuelle Hochschule Bayern (VHB)*, the virtual higher education system of Bavaria, which "promotes and coordinates the use and development of multimedia teaching and learning in Bavaria".[11]

The universal trend to adopt digital tools in higher education put an emphasis on *learning* and consequently a more active role of the learner in a great variety of approaches; however, new technologies applied by teachers usually supported a continuation of expository teaching, albeit in modern forms, as shown by the findings of Zemsky and Massy (2004) in the United States. As a result, the distinctive feature of distance education in pre-digital times—of *mediating* teaching and learning as opposed to direct teaching and learning relations in conventional classroom settings—almost disappeared. New media and digital technologies captured all areas in higher education and former differentiators became in blended teaching and learning scenarios, with evermore variations of expository teaching and independent learning as the basic form of public higher education in the digital era.

---

[11] Translated from: http://www.vhb.org/startseite/ [30.08.2016].

Only a few universities and some specialized institutions of applied sciences (just as the *Wissenschaftsrat* had recommended emphatically in 1992) developed and continued to offer dedicated distance education programs reaching out to students located at a distance from the institution. The *Hochschulkompass* lists a total of 264 distance education degree-granting programs (undergraduate and continuing education) in 2016 at state universities in Germany (data as at 8th September 2016).[12] Their professional association is the *DGWF* (the German Association for University Continuing and Distance Education[13]). It is a hallmark of these institutions to demonstrate low-cost-and-high-outcome solutions in distance education and training (Bernath and Hülsmann 2004). The most radical and comprehensive distance education scenario showcasing the advancements of the electronic age (launched in 2000) is the fully online *Master of Distance Education* program offered jointly by *Carl von Ossietzky University of Oldenburg* and the *University of Maryland University College (UMUC)* in the United States (Bernath and Rubin 2003; Hülsmann and Bernath 2010).

The *FernUniversität* in Hagen continues to apply the distance education model with print-based distance-teaching materials, increasingly embellished with online components, thus carefully transforming teaching and learning modes into online distance education. The *FernUniversität* dissolved regional student support centers in collaboration with conventional universities and provides student support all by themselves. The *Zentrales Institut für Fernstudienforschung (ZIFF)*, the central institute for distance education research at the *FernUniversität*, once a hallmark and highly regarded internationally, was closed in 2006. Seminal works by the most outstanding researchers remain treasured, for example Peters (1998, 2010) and Holmberg (1986, 2005), as well as the series of 126 volumes, edited by the *ZIFF* comprising all relevant aspects of distance education and authored by almost everyone of distinction in the field.[14]

Current Regulatory Framework for Open and Distance Learning in Germany

The 16 German *Länder* (states) have authority over their respective education systems, hence 16 different sets of laws and regulations need to be taken into consideration. Detailed statements of these laws can be found in the *Deutsches Hochschulrahmengesetz (HRG[15])*, the German higher education framework law, the *Landeshochschulgesetze (LHG[16])*, the university laws of each federal state, and the

[12]http://www.hochschulkompass.de/studium/suche/erweiterte-suche [08.09.2016].

[13]https://dgwf.net/arbeitsgemeinschaften/ag-f/ueber-die-ag-f/ [01.09.2016].

[14]ZIFF-Papers: https://ub-deposit.fernuni-hagen.de/servlets/solr/find?q=ZIFF+Papiere [04.09.2016].

[15]http://www.bmbf.de/pub/HRG_20050126.pdf [18.07.2016].

[16]https://www.hrk.de/themen/hochschulsystem/hochschulrecht/ [25.08.2016].

Gesetz zum Schutz der Teilnehmer am Fernunterricht—Fernunterrichtsschutzgesetz (FernUSG[17])—the law of the protection of participants in distance learning.

Promulgated in 1977, the *FernUSG* defines in detail the requirements that a program must meet in order to be accepted as a distance learning offering. The *FernUSG* defines *Fernunterricht* as "contractually imparting for profit knowledge and skills, when teacher and learner are exclusively or predominantly separated and when the teacher or an authorized person are monitoring the learning outcome" (*FernUSG*, § 1(1)). Since this law is derived from the laws for consumer protection, it is obligatory for *private* distance teaching enterprises. There is an ongoing debate as to whether these regulations should also be applied to *public* universities, particularly in the case of marketed, fee-charging courses and programs.[18] In recent years, alongside the growing activities of universities in the field of further education and professional training, the introduction of the ISO 29990[19] as an international quality standard for learning services has also influenced the debate on quality standards in higher distance education.

Among the 16 federal state documents on university laws, 13 explicitly mention distance education as a possible mode of delivery. However, none of them contain a special section about programs offered entirely at a distance. The general understanding for all university laws and regulations is the traditional campus-based setting. Distance education is therefore seen as an additional offer or variation, which is not intended to replace campus-based programs. Most universities therefore use a blended learning approach as a framework for their online offers. In accordance with the *Deutsches Hochschulrahmengesetz (HRG[20])*—which states that credits obtained from distance education courses may be recognized in traditional undergraduate and graduate degree settings [Section 13(2)]—more universities have recently expanded their programs to target new groups besides 'traditional' students. However, as most statements on university distance education are linked primarily to the fields of continuing education and professional training, these areas continue to be more relevant for teaching at a distance in Germany's public higher education sector.

---

[17]http://www.gesetze-im-internet.de/fernusg/ [18.08.2016].

[18]Critique and reply on the Law of the Protection of Participants in Distance Learning (S. 765 ff.): http://www.zfu.de/files/Mitteilungen/alte_Mitteilungen_der_ZFU.pdf [24.07.2016].

[19]http://www.beuth.de/ce/norm/din-iso-29990/135409271 [25.08.2016].

[20]http://www.bmbf.de/pub/HRG_20050126.pdf [18.08.2016].

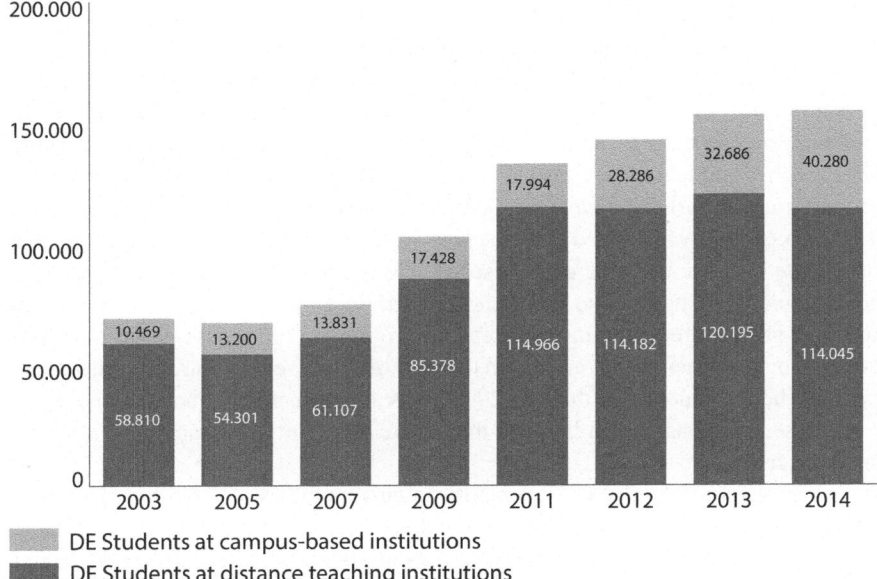

Fig. 1 Numbers of participants in distance and e-learning programs from 2003 to 2014 [based on *Forum DistancE-Learning, Fernunterrichtsstatistik*, 2014 (http://www.forum-distance-learning.de/ fernunterrichtstatistik [24.08.2016])]

Statistics About Students in Distance Education and Training

Figure 1 displays the numbers of participants in the sector described as *Fernstudium* (degree-granting distance higher education programs) at distance teaching institutions and campus-based universities from 2003 to 2014:

In 2014, 154,325 students were enrolled, with 114,045 of them at distance education HEIs (such as the *FernUniversität*) and a smaller proportion (40,280) in distance education programs at campus-based HEIs. Of the 114,045 students enrolled in distance education institutions in Germany in 2014, 70,632 studied at the *FernUniversität*, and 42,959 students were enrolled at private universities of applied science; both these numbers have nearly doubled since 2007.[21] And even for distance programs provided by campus-based HEIs, student numbers grew from 13,831 in 2007 to 40,280 in 2014. These latter programs are financed mainly through cost-recovering participation fees (Graeßner 2007). Of the total of 2.8 million students enrolled in all German universities and universities of applied science in 2015,[22] an estimated 1.5% were enrolled in distance education programs (*Fernstudium*). This proportion has not changed significantly since 1991 (Holm 2013, p. 108).

---

[21] http://fdlmedia.istis.de/FU-Statistik/Fernunterrichtsstatistik_2014.pdf, p. 16 [01.09.2016].
[22] https://www.bmbf.de/de/der-studierendensurvey-1036.html [18.08.2016].

The demand for flexible distance education programs in Germany is expanding. The most important reason reported by students for studying at a distance at the *FernUniversität* is the flexibility offered by distance programs (cited by 80–90% of students). Most other reasons cited are closely linked to this flexibility because all of them relate to the students' professional and/or family commitments (Stöter et al. 2014, p. 443).

State Funding of Distance Education and Related Modes of Teaching and Learning

In 2014 the Federal Government of Germany implemented the so-called *"Digitale Agenda 2014–2017"* in order to cope with the challenges in seven different policy fields, one of them being education, research, science, culture and media.[23] The aim of this agenda is to enhance the digitization of the educational system, with many funding programs being implemented in 2015. Since universities lack the resources for their own development (Kerres et al. 2012), most efforts are driven by external motivations linked to special projects funded by the government or the European Union (Hanft and Maschwitz 2012). Unfortunately, the interest of HEIs in such projects may be driven by the funds themselves, rather than by the themes and aims of the projects (Kreidl 2011). This aspect is emphasized by the indicator-based granting of funds by German states to their HEIs, since one major component of state funding is success in procuring third-party funds (Stöter 2015).

Since 1999 there have been several nationwide funding programs with a focus on the development and implementation of distance education or blended learning programs.

These large-scale programs can be viewed as the primary reason for universities to adapt and strengthen their use of distance education tools and to develop strategies for implementing the necessary infrastructure. The future of distance education in Germany, at least for the public sector, depends largely on these kinds of programs, but even more so on the strategies that institutions need to develop for sustainable implementation of the project outcomes.

Future Developments in German (Open) Distance Education

The development of the distance education sector within German HEI is driven mainly by national authorities, which support HEIs by means of various funded projects. Due to political and strategic decisions, the institutions themselves do not focus on the development of specific distance programs. But through funded projects the development of distance education programs is enhanced from outside of the institutions. In the years to come, a number of universities will have developed

---

[23] http://www.bmwi.de/DE/Themen/Digitale-Welt/digitale-agenda.html [23.08.2016].

continuing education programs based on blended learning designs, and adult students will have the opportunity to study in a format suitable for their needs; however, these courses will be subject to significant fees. The challenge will be to learn from the processes adopted by these continuing education programs, so as to enrich traditional study with distance education modes. The positive outcome is that there will be more opportunities to enrol in distance education programs for more people, especially at campus-based HEIs.

In order to provide a glimpse into possible future developments of the distance education sector in Germany, we summarize some aspects of current developments, which pose a challenge to traditional universities. The new regulations that were established in 2009, and the following years forced HEIs to adjust their programs to the needs of new target groups, in addition to the on-going struggle to cope with the growing number of 'traditional' students. Although programs for adult learners, based on blended learning designs at campus-based HEIs, have been enhanced through various initiatives, national public HEIs will need to compete against the private sector to attract students from this new target group.

From the total number of 427 universities or universities of applied sciences across Germany only a fraction provides online or blended distance education programs. Based on an analysis by the *Hochschulkompass*[24] in March 2016, a total of 198 distance education programs offered by traditional universities were identified. Of the 52 providers of distance education university programs, 36 are public universities or universities of applied sciences (86 programs) and 16 are private providers (112 programs). Nearly all the private providers offer their courses exclusively at a distance and, due to the demand for flexible study programs and the lack thereof at traditional, campus-based HEIs, this private sector has been expanding massively.

Only a few public institutions have established distinct centers for their distance education programs, which are selected by very small proportion of students, although the total numbers of enrolments are growing, so do the numbers of students in general. Most of the universities in Germany tend to continue to focus on their 'traditional' target groups and study programs, and are therefore designed with these groups in mind, remaining campus-based in general; however, the various funding-programs might foster a change.

References

Adler, H. (1990). *DDR-Fernstudium im Wandel. ZIFF Papiere, 83*. Retrieved from https://ub-deposit.fernuni-hagen.de/receive/mir_mods_00000325.
Bernath, U. (1992). Zur Stellung und zum Stellenwert der Mentorentätigkeit im Fernstudiensystem der FernUniversität Hagen. Ein Diskussionsbeitrag aus dem (nicht-nordrhein-westfälischen) Fernstudienzentrum der Carl von Ossietzky Universität Oldenburg im Jahre 1991. In N.-M. Bückmann, G. E. Ortner, & R. Schuemer (Hrsg.) *Lehre und Betreuung im Fernstudium: Abschlußbericht zum Ringkolloquium des ZIFF im Wintersemester 91/92.* FernUniversität Hagen.

---

[24]http://www.hochschulkompass.de/ [25.08.2016].

Bernath, U. (1994). The centre for distance education at Carl von Ossietzky University of Oldenburg. *Open Learning, 9*(3), 52–55. Retrieved from http://www.uni-oldenburg.de/zef/literat/centrwww.htm.

Bernath, U. (1996). Distance education in mainstream higher education: A strategic issue for central resource and developing units at conventional universities. In: M. Thompson (Ed.) *Internationalism in distance education: A vision for higher education—Selected papers from the First International Distance Education Conference* (pp. 45–51). The Pennsylvania State University: University Park. Retrieved from http://www.uni-oldenburg.de/zef/literat/mainwww.htm.

Bernath, U., & Rubin, E. (2003). The online Master of Distance Education (MDE): Its history and realization. In U. Bernath & E. Rubin (Eds.). *Reflections on teaching and learning in an online master program—A case study* (Vol. 6, pp. 9–50). Oldenburg: Bibliotheks- und Informationssystem der Carl von Ossietzky Universität Oldenburg. Retrieved from http://www.uni-oldenburg.de/en/c3l/mde/asf-series/volume-6/.

Bernath, U., & Hülsmann, T. (2004). Low cost/high outcomes approaches in open, distance and e-learning. In U. Bernath & A. Szücs (Eds.) *Supporting the learner in distance education and e-learning*. Proceedings of the Third EDEN Research Workshop, Carl von Ossietzky University of Oldenburg, Germany, March 4–6, 2004 (pp. 485–491). Oldenburg: Bibliotheks- und Informationssystem der Universität Oldenburg.

Daniel, Sir J. (2016). Making Sense of blended learning: treasuring an older tradition or finding a better future? Published in *teachonline.ca* (http://teachonline.ca). Retrieved April 23, 2016 from http://teachonline.ca/tools-trends/blended-learning-successful-design-delivery-and-student-engagement/making-sense-blended-learning-treasuring-older-tradition-or-finding-better-future.

Delling, R. M. (1978). *Briefwechsel als Bestandteil und Vorläufer des Fernstudiums. ZIFF Papiere, 19*. Retrieved from http://deposit.fernuni-hagen.de/1735/1/ZP_019.pdf#page=25&zoom=auto,-12,816.

Deutsches Institut für Fernstudien an der Universität Tübingen (Ed.). (1981). *Versuch für das Fernstudium im Medienverbund. Abschlußbericht und Stellungnahmen*. Tübingen: DIFF.

Dieckmann, H., & Zinn, H. (2016). *Die Geschichte des Fernunterrichts in Deutschland*. Manuscript submitted for publication.

Dohmen, G. (1968). *Der Aufbau des Hochschulfernstudiums in der Bundesrepublik, Tübinger Plan*. Tübinger Beiträge zum Fernstudium (Vol. 1). Weinheim: Beltz.

Graeßner, G. (2007). Preisgestaltung und Finanzierung von Hochschulweiterbildung unter Berücksichtigung rechtlicher Rahmenbedingungen. In A. Hanft & A. Simmel (Eds.): *Vermarktung von Hochschulweiterbildung: Theorie und Praxis* (pp. 159–174). Münster: Waxmann.

Greven, J. (Ed.). (1998). *Das Funkkolleg 1966–1998. Ein Modell wissenschaftlicher Weiterbildung im Medienverbund*. Weinheim: Beltz.

Groten, H. (1992). The role of study centres at the Fernuniversität. *Open Learning, 7*(1), 50–56.

Hanft, A., & Maschwitz, A. (2012). Verankerung von Lebenslangem Lernen an Hochschulen—Ein internationaler Vergleich. In *Hessische Blätter für Volksbildung. Wissenschaftliche Weiterbildung, 2/2012* (pp. 113–124). Retrieved from https://www.uni-oldenburg.de/fileadmin/user_upload/paedagogik-web/HBV1202_Beitrag_Hanft__Maschwitz-1.pdf.

Holm, P. D. J.-M. (2013). Fernstudium und lebenslanges Lernen. In: A. Papmehl & H. J. Tümmers (Eds.), *Die Arbeitswelt im 21. Jahrhundert* (pp. 107–124). Wiesbaden: Springer Fachmedien. Retrieved from http://link.springer.com/chapter/10.1007/978-3-658-01416-2_8.

Holmberg, B. (1986). *Growth and structure of distance education*. London: Croom Helm.

Holmberg, B. (1995). The evolution of the character and practice of distance education. In *Open Learning, 10*(2), 47–53; reprinted in Holmberg, B. (2001). *Distance education in essence: An overview of theory and practice in the early twenty-first century* (Vol. 4). Bibliotheks-und Informationssystem der Carl von Ossietzky Universität Oldenburg (BIS). Retrieved from http://www.uni-oldenburg.de/en/c3l/mde/asf-series/volume-4/.

Holmberg, B. (2005). *The evolution, principles and practices of distance education* (Vol. 11). Bibliotheks-und Informationssystem der Carl von Ossietzky Universität Oldenburg (BIS). Retrieved from: http://www.uni-oldenburg.de/en/c3l/mde/asf-series/volume-11/.

Hülsmann, T., & Bernath, U. (2010). Knowledge Management as professional development: The case of the MDE. In J. Liebowitz & M. S. Frank (Eds.), *Knowledge management and e-learning* (pp. 253–271). Boca Raton, London, New York: CRC Press.

Kappel, H.-H., Lehmann, B., & Loeper, J. (2002). Distance education at conventional universities in Germany. *The International Review of Research in Open and Distributed Learning (IRRODL)*, 2(2). Retrieved from: http://www.irrodl.org/index.php/irrodl/article/view/62/127.

Kerres, M., Hanft, A., Wilkesmann, U., & Wolff-Bendik, K. (Eds.). (2012). *Studium 2020. Positionen und Perspektiven zum lebenslangen Lernen an Hochschulen*. Münster: Waxmann.

Kreidl, C. (2011). *Akzeptanz und Nutzung von E-Learning-Elementen an Hochschulen: Gründe für die Einführung und Kriterien der Anwendung von E-Learning*. Münster: Waxmann.

Mandl, H., Stein, N., & Trabasso, T. (Eds.). (1984). *Learning and comprehension of text*. Hillsdale, New York: Erlbaum.

Möhle, H. (1986). *Aus- und Weiterbildung Erwachsener auf Hochschulebene in der DDR. ZIFF Papiere*, 64. FernUniversität Hagen. Retrieved from https://ub-deposit.fernuni-hagen.de/receive/mir_mods_00000305.

Möhle, H. (1990). *Neue Entwicklungen im Fernstudium der DDR. ZIFF Papiere*, 80. FernUniversität Hagen. Retrieved from https://ub-deposit.fernuni-hagen.de/receive/mir_mods_00000322.

Moore, M. G., & Kearsley, G. (1996). *Distance education: A systems view of online learning*. Belmont: Wadsworth.

Peters, O. (1967). *Das Fernstudium an Universitäten und Hochschulen*. Weinheim: Beltz.

Peters, O. (1992). Some observations on dropping out in distance education. *Distance Education*, 13(2), 234–269; see the original article in German: Anmerkungen zum Studienabbruch (Some Remarks about Students' Dropout). *ZIFF Papiere* 73, Nov 1988. Retrieved from http://files.eric.ed.gov/fulltext/ED316228.pdf.

Peters, O. (2001). *Learning and teaching in distance education. Analyses and interpretations from an international perspective*. London: Routledge.

Peters, O. (2010). *Distance education in transition. Developments and issues* (Vol. 5). Bibliotheks- und Informationssystem der Carl von Ossietzky Universität Oldenburg (BIS). Retrieved from http://www.uni-oldenburg.de/en/c3l/mde/asf-series/volume-5/.

Stöter, J. (2015). Germany case study. In: A. Owusu-Boampong & C. Holmberg (Eds.). *Distance education offer of European higher education institutions—The potential*. Report 3 (of 3) of the IDEAL (Impact of Distance Education on Adult Learning) project. Retrieved from https://idealprojectblog.files.wordpress.com/2015/07/ideal_germany-case-study2.pdf.

Stöter, J., Bullen, M., Zawacki-Richter, O., & von Prümmer, C. (2014). From the back door into the mainstream—learner characteristics in the context of lifelong learning. In O. Zawacki-Richter & T. Anderson (Eds.), *Online distance education—Towards a research agenda*. Athabasca, Edmonton, Canada: Athabasca University Press.

Wissenschaftsrat. (1992). *Empfehlungen zum Fernstudium, Drs. 929/92, Nov 13, 1992*. Retrieved from www.wissenschaftsrat.de/download/archiv/929-92.pdf.

Zawacki-Richter, O., von Prümmer, C., & Stöter, J. (2015). Open Universities: Offener Zugang zur Hochschule in nationaler und internationaler Perspektive. In *Beiträge zur Hochschulforschung 37*. Bayerisches Staatsinstitut für Hochschulforschung und Hochschulplanung (IHF) (pp. 8–24). München.

Zemsky, R., & Massy, W.F. (2004). *Thwarted innovation. What happened to e-learning and why?* The Learning Alliance at the University of Pennsylvania. Retrieved from: http://www.immagic.com/eLibrary/ARCHIVES/GENERAL/UPENN_US/P040600Z.pdf.

Germany—Commentary

Burkhard Lehmann

In just a few pages, Bernath and Stöter have offered a comprehensive overview of the emergence and development of distance education in Germany, one that describes in detail all the important milestones and structural elements in the history of distance education, from its early beginnings to the present day. The way in which they describe the conflicting and often extreme circumstances under which distance education in Germany has developed is particularly instructive, as is their observation that German distance education originated in the non-academic field and entered the world of academic education at a relatively late stage. One of the unique features of German distance education and its historical development is that, because the country was divided into two German states, there were two different approaches: a socialist-style of distance education in the east and a more western-style distance education in the west. It goes without saying that the socialist-style system of distance learning was no longer viable following the reunification of the two German states, and its demise was inevitable. Another factor highlighted by Bernath and Stöter is that distance education is divided into state (public) and private (commercial) sectors.

The entry of a host of commercial providers into the distance education sector lends support to the entrepreneurial notion that there is money to be earned with distance learning. This view appears to be based on the observation that distance education can achieve economies of scale that are impossible with on-campus teaching, as the latter is perceived and operated as a personnel-intensive service. In comparison, media-based teaching seems inexpensive to produce, as long as high turnover figures can be achieved. Growth rates in Germany are currently between four and six per cent, which is a further indicator of the economic appeal of distance education.

B. Lehmann (✉)
Center for Distance Learning and University Continuing Education, University of Koblenz-Landau, Mainz, Germany
e-mail: lehmann@uni-koblenz.de

© The Author(s) 2018
A. Qayyum and O. Zawacki-Richter (eds.), *Open and Distance Education in Australia, Europe and the Americas*, SpringerBriefs in Open and Distance Education,
https://doi.org/10.1007/978-981-13-0298-5_9

Within academic discourse, distance education is often described as a form of self-directed learning, and it has been argued that this form of education reflects all of the different learning theory approaches that have emerged over time from education research. Bernath and Stöter offer a different interpretation, which stems from their interpretation of distance education as a form of adult education learning and teaching format that requires its own, separate discursive evaluation.

The authors then examine in detail the *FernUniversität* in Hagen—the leading distance education institution in Germany. This is no surprise, as the *FernUniversität* is not just Germany's largest higher education institution, but is also the only German university to offer its programmes entirely in a distance-learning format with distinct faculties for its programmes. In the same way that Britain's Open University was the role model for many of the world's distance education institutions, Hagen's university provided the blueprint for numerous distance learning providers within Germany. However, it must be added that the *FernUniversität* is a "bare bones" or special-interest university, as it offers a limited range of subjects within only four departments: Law, Economics, Mathematics and Computer Science and Cultural and Social Sciences.

With the founding of the *FernUniversität*, it is interesting to note that, from an education policy perspective, a project was implemented that had its origins in higher education policy ideas and reform plans of social democracy. This is an interesting parallel to England, where here, too, the Open University was one of the global flagships of distance education and owes its existence to the efforts of social democrats, specifically the Labour Party under Harold Wilson. In both cases, the universities were founded as politically-motivated projects aimed at establishing more equal opportunities for promoting social inclusion.

Although Germany's distance education sector is characterized by a growing momentum, when compared to on-campus study, the actual format of distance education plays only a minor role in this developing dynamic. The statistics provided by Bernath and Stöter clearly show that distance education is only the second most popular form of education in Germany, an occurrence also reflected in other parts of the world. Despite increasing demand for distance education in recent years, as well as higher acceptance levels, the dominant format is still the traditional face-to-face style of education. Ever since their first development over 800 years ago, universities have been attendance-based institutions, which continues to be the case today. Distance learning is merely an additional, alternative option for specific target groups.

In Germany, too, the emergence of digital educational media (which researchers refer to as a new generation of distance-education) has caused the boundaries between distance and on-campus learning to become increasingly indistinct and blurred. For example, in the terminology it is no longer possible to clearly distinguish between "distance", "online education" and "blended learning". Certain educational organizations are now offering online courses or online degree courses without linking them in any way to the concept of distance education and its traditions. Even the *FernUniversität* is committed to the concept of "Blended Learning".

However, digitalisation has also given a new boost to distance education in Germany. Bernath and Stöter note that, in addition to the numerous government support schemes that have been launched to promote internet technology use, e-learning has also been given a new lease of life in recent years through the advent of MOOCs (massive open online courses), which make distance teaching and learning more attractive. IT-based distance education offers considerable improvements in the areas of interaction and communication, which is also a huge benefit. Not only will the impact of digital technology fundamentally change distance education in Germany, it will also require adjustments to be made at a statutory level. In this context, Germany's unique Distance Learning Protection Act, which was designed for an analogous rather than digital distance-education world, is an obsolete model and in dire need of reform.

United Kingdom

Anne Gaskell

Introduction

For nearly 160 years, the United Kingdom (UK) has provided Higher Education (HE) opportunities to students learning at a distance. The University of London (UoL), founded in 1826, was the first University to offer truly distance teaching from 1858, when the residential requirements previously in place for Universities were abandoned. Over a hundred years later in 1969, The Open University UK (OU), still the UK's only single-mode distance teaching institution, received its Royal Charter.

However, the picture in the UK is not straightforward. The UK's four countries (England, Scotland, Wales and Northern Ireland) share some aspects of regulation and quality assurance but have differences in terms of funding arrangements and accountability. For example, the UK's Quality Code for Higher Education (QAA 2012) covers all four countries, but Scotland has devolved responsibilities for its implementation which have led to distinctive features in its Quality Enhancement Framework. HE funding is also distributed through different national assemblies and funding councils.

The overall UK picture is of online, distance and e-learning (ODeL) gaining increasing respect and acceptance. There have also been substantial changes over the century and a half. These have been particularly important from the 1970s with the immediate success of the OU, from the 1990s with the growth of Information and Communication Technologies (ICTs), and from the 1990s onwards with major changes in Government funding for tuition and part-time students.

A. Gaskell (✉)
Independent Distance Education Consultant, Milton Keynes, UK
e-mail: Annegaskell@outlook.com

© The Author(s) 2018   85
A. Qayyum and O. Zawacki-Richter (eds.), *Open and Distance Education in Australia, Europe and the Americas*, SpringerBriefs in Open and Distance Education,
https://doi.org/10.1007/978-981-13-0298-5_10

The History of UK Distance and Online Education

In 1859 the weekly periodical *All The Year Round* described the recently available UoL External Programme as "The English People's University" through its revolutionary provision of distance learning opportunities for the "young shoemaker in his garret" (Kenyon Jones 2008, p. 21). Students could pay the registration fee and prepare themselves to sit UoL examinations in whatever way they chose. Many studied in isolation or with private tuition, but increasingly from the 1880s through correspondence colleges which provided a range of support services, including exam preparation (ibid. pp. 163–4). The absence of residential requirements was not the only unusual feature of UoL external study: from 1878 for the first time in the UK, University degrees were open to women.

External study was also available overseas, particularly within the then British Colonies. In 1864 Mauritius received special permission to hold UoL exams and by 1882 there were 17 'colonial' centres rising to 53 in 29 countries in 1943. By 2008 there were students or alumni in 180 of the world's 192 countries (Kenyon Jones, p. 48). Initially the impetus for these developments may have been the "imperial mission" of UoL; The Council for External Studies in 1910, for example argued that:

> The far-reaching and imperial character of the work at present conducted by the External Side of the University of London, the wide range of subjects… and the high standards… constitute it a national necessity which cannot be replaced by any other education system. (Kenyon Jones 2008, p. 193)

While there were inherent inequalities in the lack of support for learners, UoL's External Programme provided widely available opportunity and an exemplar for curriculum design and quality assurance unheard of in distance education at the time (Tait 2008). Only in the 1960s did internal students begin to outnumber external students in the University. UoL's International Programmes (formerly External Studies) still has a global mission to provide high quality education to students across the world.

The opportunities provided by the OU from 1971 immediately appealed to large numbers who had been unable to study at higher level. Many of these were teachers seeking to gain a degree for what was becoming a graduate profession, but many others were attracted by the OU's mission: "open as to people, places, methods and ideas" and especially to the OU's unique lack of entry requirements at undergraduate level.

The OU also pioneered entirely new methods of teaching and learning at a distance, many of which have been adopted world-wide. Multi-media course materials included high quality printed teaching units, radio programmes, TV programmes (broadcast originally at peak viewing times) and Home Experiment Kits for those studying science subjects. In addition, there was a comprehensive network of student support established through 13 Regional Centres which appointed local tutors and support staff and organised local tutorials, exam centres and degree ceremonies.

The development of online resources within the OU since the 1990s has had a major impact on some of the original teaching and support structures. In particular, various functions that were distributed are now being centralised. In November 2015 the OU's Council supported the closure of seven of the 10 English regional centres; one had already been closed, and the remaining two have changed their function. From 2018, the OU works mainly through three national centres in Edinburgh, Cardiff and Belfast and the central campus in Milton Keynes.

In Scotland, the University of the Highlands and Islands (UHI) provides a relatively recent example of undergraduate flexible learning, enabling students to gain degrees solely through online learning since 1995. UHI offers a spectrum of courses ranging from fully on-campus to fully online and has a particular mission to "provide access to all members of the region's community to new forms of education opportunity... [whose members are] geographically spread and often located in small and demographically scattered rural island communities" (Smith and Macdonald 2015, p. 24). UHI provides both Further Education (FE) and HE and is delivered by a network of thirteen academic partners spread across the Highlands and Islands, Moray and Perthshire. This is an area of some 17,000 square miles, over one sixth of the UK's land mass. The geographical range "was a primary driver of the adoption of blended learning" for UHI (Panciroli et al. 2015, p. 39). Although many programmes are campus-based, or combine online with Video Conferencing or face-to-face teaching, UHI's online courses can be accessed entirely through the internet. Approximately 15% of UHI students currently study on fully online programmes.

These examples from some of the undergraduate ODeL providers in the UK indicate their differences in scope and mission; UoL aims for a global impact, the OU retains its mission for social justice, still largely in the UK and UHI focuses particularly on geographically remote students in the Scottish Highlands and Islands. All three institutions also have active research departments, perhaps most notably the OU's Institute of Educational Technology (IET) which is still the only UK HE research department solely concerned with ODeL.

Developments in ODeL from the 1990s transformed distance teaching in the UK in two main ways. Firstly through the introduction of online platforms for administrative and student support and the provision of some teaching resources which have now been adopted by all UK HEIs. Online support in these areas varies, but can enable learners to access teaching materials and recorded lectures online, undertake all administrative matters, and engage with fellow students, and in some cases tutors/lecturers, via forums, email and messaging boards. Secondly, while there are still universities like Oxbridge that emphasise the importance of face-to-face contact, there are increasing numbers of modules or courses, particularly at Masters level which are taught exclusively online or at a distance.

In 2010, the Higher Education Funding Council for England (Hefce) commissioned a study to provide a broad overview of UK HE ODeL—defined as "any course, at any HE academic level, delivered to students at a distance from the host institution, which had a significant component delivered online" (White et al. 2010, p. 10). The findings were significant: the vast majority of ODeL provision was at postgraduate level; much of it was developed at departmental level on an ad hoc basis; most could be described as continuing professional development; and there was no reliable or accurate information available about provision of ODeL "much of which remains hidden in labyrinthine institutional websites" (White et al. 2010, p. 1). However, the data collected "identified over 2600 HE level online and distance learning courses offered by, or on behalf of, UK HE and FE institutions". These included:

- 1,528 courses offered by 113 HE and FE institutions; of which 510 were identified as being delivered online (including blended learning);
- 952 courses offered by the Open University; of which 600 were dependent on the web and a further 95 were delivered fully online;
- 175 courses offered in partnership with commercial partners (White et al. 2010 p. 12).

With the exception of a few Higher Education Institutions (HEIs), UoL and the OU, ODeL provision still remains largely at postgraduate level and involves relatively small numbers, although there is increasing institutional support for new developments. The University of Edinburgh, for example, offers 67 fully online postgraduate degrees which do not require any campus attendance. There are no exams—technology has enabled a check on the online footprint of a student to ensure authorship of essays and dissertations, and degrees can be awarded through a Second Life online ceremony. The University of Leicester offers over 60 postgraduate courses, most of them part-time. Many other Universities offer ODeL for post-graduate niche markets; for example the University of Belfast offers Pharmacy, Cardiff University offers Medical Education. These courses generally attract relatively low numbers, often around 20 or fewer students.

There have also been notable failures, for example the UK e-University which was established in 2001 as a single vehicle for the delivery of UK universities' HE programmes over the internet, but was wound up in 2004 by Hefce "having spent £50 million of public money but having succeeded only in attracting 900 students" (House of Commons 2005, p. 3). This failure was attributed to a number of factors: an approach that was supply-driven rather than demand-led, an inability to form partnerships between the public and private sectors, insufficient market research, too much concentration on e-learning platforms, and "an over-confident presumption about the scale of the demand for wholly internet-based e-learning"(House of Commons 2005, p. 3). In 2002 *Scottish Knowledge* had also closed. This had involved 13 Scottish Universities and eight colleges and had aimed to make a major impact on the global online education market (Smith and Macdonald 2015).

Funding

Most UK ODeL is delivered through government-funded Universities. Before 1992, these, and specialist HEIs were funded through one UK-wide Universities Funding Council; the one exception being the OU, which was funded directly from the Department of Education and Science (DES). The UK Further and Higher Education Act 1992 had a major impact—some of which was to create a more unified HE system; for example:

- Former polytechnics became universities
- The OU became part of mainstream higher education funding
- The Quality Assurance Agency (QAA) and the Higher Education Statistics Agency (HESA) were created with oversight of all HEI provision in the UK.

However, separate funding councils were created for England, Scotland and Wales, and later for Northern Ireland, all with devolved powers for funding HE in their countries. These have gained increased importance since the creation of three national assemblies in 1998.

In England HE funding is allocated by the Department for Education and distributed through Hefce, in Scotland through the Scottish Funding Council (SFC), in Wales through the Higher Education Funding Council of Wales (HEFCW), and in Northern Ireland through the Department for Employment and Learning (DELNI).

Until 1998, full-time campus-based students at all UK HEIs did not have to pay for tuition and could apply for maintenance grants. In 1998, means-tested tuition fees were introduced, initially UK-wide, but now devolved to the separate funding councils, and grants were converted into loans. However, these measures did not apply to part-time distance or online learners, who had to pay their own fees and were not eligible for grants, or loans when introduced.

Measures introduced since 1998 in England have had a major impact. In 2004 means-tested government grants became available for part-time students for the first time. However, in 2007 the government phased out support for any student studying for a qualification that was equivalent to or lower than a qualification they had previously gained, and this particularly affected the OU and Birkbeck College, UoL, both of which had large numbers of mature students aiming to change career: "The number of Britons starting part-time undergraduate degrees fell by 40 per cent between 2010–2013" (Weinbren 2015, p. 170).

From 2010, part-time students became eligible for student loans on the same basis as full-time students, but teaching budgets to all Universities were cut by 80%, and the government formally withdrew all funding for the arts, humanities and social sciences. This again has had a major impact in terms of rising fees: the OU now (March 2018) has variable fees across the four nations but charges £5728 for a full-time equivalent year for a B.A. or B.Sc. (Hons) in England. This may compare favourably with the 2018 government cap on full-time student tuition fees (£9250—currently under review) but is still considerably higher than earlier fees. In Scotland, however, the tuition fees for academic year 2017–18 are £1820 for a full-time first degree for eligible students (SFC 2017). Scottish HE students are in general funded more generously than English HE students. Students on UoL International Programmes have always been entirely self-funded.

Funding and costs for all distance and online HE in the UK are therefore largely dependent on the policies of UK Government and national Funding Councils.

ODeL and UK HE Provision

With the exception of UoL International Progammes and the OU, government-funded ODeL is mostly located within campus-based, residential HEIs and so is treated on equal terms with other HEIs in relation to QA and devolved funding arrangements.

However, there are some exceptions. There is a relatively limited number of private HE providers which include the University of Buckingham, the only private University in the UK; BPP University, the first publicly owned company in the UK which obtained degree awarding powers in 2007 and is dedicated solely to business and the professions; and Pearson College where courses are designed, developed and delivered by industry. All of these can include online and distance elements but are not primarily ODeL providers.

Even though ODeL providers are well recognised among HEIs, UK University "League tables" often do not include the OU because many of the questions are related to campus-based facilities. *The Guardian*'s League tables, for example, include 121 Universities but not the OU. This can give a skewed vision of UK HE—and especially ODeL—provision, despite the fact that the OU is included in the UK's National Student Survey (NSS http://www.hefce.ac.uk/lt/nss/results/). However, these surveys may not always accurately convey the experience or achievements of ODeL students and it has been argued that revised surveys should be developed (Ashby et al. 2011).

The Popularity of ODeL? Student Enrolments

Student enrolments in ODeL over 150 years have related mainly to social context and governmental funding. The UoL's External Programme, for example, saw marked increases in registrations during World War Two as the only available possibility of study for many; numbers rose from about 10,000 in 1939 to over 16,000 in 1945 (Kenyon Jones p. 86). In 2007 over 41,000 students were studying with the London External Programme, only 12% of whom were based in the UK (Kenyon Jones 2008, p. 48).

The OU enrolled its first students in 1971 when 41,000 people applied to study for undergraduate degrees, 32,287 were offered a place and 24,220 accepted. Student numbers were capped by the government at the time because of limits on funding: "Over the next decade OU student numbers grew in line, not with applications but with funding of places" (Weinbren 2015, p. 167). By 1980 there were 61,000 undergraduates and by 1990 over 72,622 (ibid. p. 168). With the relaxation of the government cap on student numbers, the OU grew substantially, reaching a peak of over 260,000 students by 2010–11.

Enrolments on ODeL programmes remain difficult to assess. However, there are some indications and trends available.

ODeL has always been attractive to students who want to study part time, either because they have other commitments, jobs, families, caring responsibilities; or for other reasons, for example finance, disability, service in the Armed Forces, prison sentence. The most recent UK statistics show that the number of part-time students in the UK has dropped substantially since University fees were raised. In 2010–2011 there were 824,000 part-time students; and this had dropped by 21% in 2012–13 when full-time annual fees rose from £3600 to £9000 and has continued declining ever since—so that numbers of part-time students had reduced by almost a third to 570,000 in 2014–15 (HESA 2016) (Fig. 1).

Numbers of part-time students have continued to drop, by as much as 56% in the five years to 2017, and this has been attributed to the lack of government support for part-time students (The Guardian 2017).

Not all part-time students will be online or distance learners—although 76% of the OU's students have worked full or part-time during their studies—and there will be many other students who are carers and study part-time. However, the OU has been particularly badly affected. In 2016, The Times Higher Education Supplement (THES) reported that the OU's latest accounts "show that it ran up a £7.2 million deficit in 2014–15, on the back of a £16.9 million shortfall the year before. This came as the total number of students signed up for OU courses fell by 13,449 (7.2%) year-on-year, to 173,889. From a high of 260,119 learners in 2009–10, the OU has now shed a third of its enrolment in the space of six years" (THES 2016a).

The Higher Education Statistics Agency (HESA) includes data about all HE students by HE provider, level of study, mode of study and domicile and the data is not encouraging for the OU (Fig. 2).

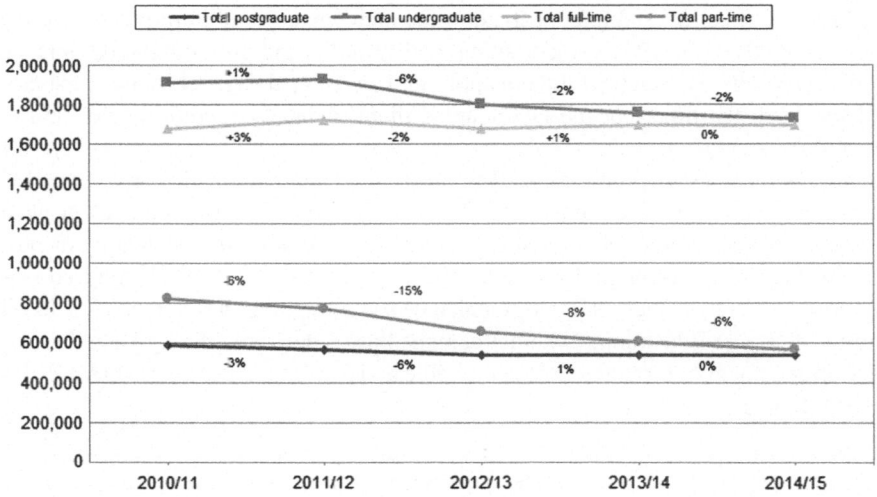

Fig. 1 UK HE student enrolments by level of study and mode of study. *Source* HESA (2016) *Statistical First Release*, 2014–15

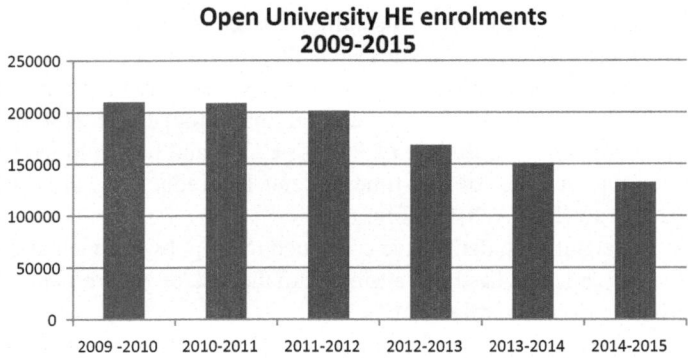

Fig. 2 Open University HE Enrolments 2009–2015. *Source* HESA (2016)

Quality Assurance

One measure of the changing acceptance and respect accorded to OdeL in the UK is that the UK's Quality Assurance Agency (QAA) is now entrusted with assuring quality and standards across all accredited UK higher education programmes, wherever, and in whatever medium they are studied. The QAA is independent of government and HEIs and acts in the public interest; this has ensured that HE ODeL is regarded as a reputable medium of delivery.

The forerunner to the QAA, the Higher Education Quality Council, HEQC, had been established in 1993 to contribute to the maintenance and improvement of the quality of HE in the UK by undertaking quality audits and providing good practice guidelines. These Guidelines did not apply, and were not always relevant to, distance education at the time, but the OU adapted them to satisfy funding bodies and to ensure its own QA approaches.

In 1999, the QAA produced draft guidelines specifically for distance education which aimed "to provide advice, mainly to campus-based institutions, about what needs to be considered when assuring the quality and academic standards of programmes provided through distance learning" (Mills 1999, p. 83). The revised version in 2010 noted that technology-enhanced learning was now embedded in all forms of Higher Education, "whether campus-based, delivered through a collaborative arrangement or through modes of flexible and distributed learning" (QAA 2010, p. 16). It also notes that:

> Recent developments in learning that uses information and communications technologies ('e-learning'), have given rise in some quarters to the belief that this approach requires an entirely separate and distinct form of quality assurance. While it is true that some technical aspects of e-modes of learning do require particular ways of meeting specific challenges, it is nonetheless also the case that most of the questions that need to be asked, and answered, about academic management are common to both e-learning and other FDL methods, and may be considered under the headings of delivery, support and assessment. (QAA 2010, p. 58)

The QAA is responsible for publishing and maintaining the UK *Quality Code for Higher Education,* conducting evidence-based external review of higher education providers and advising government on applications for degree awarding powers and the right to be called a University. The *Quality Code* covers all four nations of the UK and all international locations where UK Higher Education is provided. Its aim is to "to safeguard the academic standards of UK higher education; to assure the quality of the learning opportunities that UK higher education offers to students; to promote continuous and systematic improvement in UK higher education; [and] to ensure that information about UK higher education is publicly available." (QAA 2012, p. 1) HE review of providers and programmes, in whatever medium they are delivered, is conducted by external peer reviewers, including students (QAA 2016).

Although largely delivered by UK HEIs and mainly at HE level, Massive Open Online Courses (MOOCs) are not covered by the Quality Code: "UK universities and other awarding organisations are responsible for the quality of all the courses they offer. Since MOOCs are typically non-credit bearing and have no particular entry requirements, they are not formally scrutinised during QAA review" (QAA 2014).

What Are the Issues? What Is the Future?

Four main challenges for the future of traditional ODeL in the UK reviewed here are:

- The increasing convergence of distance and campus-based HE
- Student numbers and Government funding in the UK
- Retention rates in ODeL
- Informal learning.

In addition, changing political contexts for the UK in its relationship with the EU and the rest of the world may impact on ODeL.

As early as 1999, Tait and Mills wrote of the convergence of distance and conventional education: "We see in fact such sharp erosion of the distinction between distance education and innovative learning strategies based on the new information communication technologies (ICTs), that the continued existence of the distance education tradition must now be in question" (Tait and Mills 1999, p. 2). Tait has since argued that distance learning as a separate mode of provision is now debatable: all HEIs now use ICTs to support or deliver learning at a distance; flexible provision is the norm. What distinguishes HEIs is their mission, not their location and provision on campus or at a distance (Tait 2016).

Flexible provision is certainly increasingly available for formal teaching and learning programmes across the UK, but with the exception of UoL, the OU and UHI is mainly at Masters level. In the future, perhaps all UK HEIs will move further into undergraduate ODeL provision, as modules within a campus-based degree, or as the sole mode of delivery. If this happens, there will be increasing competition for the OU, the UK's sole single-mode ODeL provider, which has already seen a dramatic decrease in student numbers. One issue for the future is whether single-mode distance teaching institutions can survive. Will the OU's open access mission enable it to maintain student numbers and funding?

Additional challenges relate to government policies towards ODeL and HE generally. The withdrawal of funding from Arts and Social Sciences subjects was introduced in 2010 but with delayed implementation. The full impact of this policy is only now being felt in terms of increased fees. The resulting drop in part-time student numbers affects the OU already and may affect all ODeL in the future.

Student drop-out is also of key importance, particularly for the students concerned, but also for HE providers. Student retention has always been an issue for ODeL, which generally has lower rates than campus-based study, but becomes even more important when UK HE funding is increasingly limited and depends on successful student completion. Statistics are not easy to uncover, but HESA's data on non-continuation of part-time first-degree students two years after their year of entry are revealing. In 2011–12, only 2.3% of the University of Durham students had left HE compared with 43.6 percent of the OU's students. The OU's non-continuation rates were still comparable with those of Plymouth (42.9%) and Sheffield (44.4%), and do not take account of the OU's open entry policies (HESA 2013). However, these figures do not include those who leave within 50 days of beginning to study and as Simpson demonstrated for the OU in 2004, nearly 13% left before course start, and some 36% before the first assignment (usually within the 50 days of HESA data) (Simpson 2004, p. 83).

These points highlight issues for ODeL in the UK and UK HE generally, for example the dependence on government funding. Will UK HEIs be able to find additional sources of funding for ODeL if necessary? Student satisfaction is also of key importance: how far is ODeL regarded by students as a satisfactory experience compared to campus-based HEI study? The OU previously had very high scores in the Student Satisfaction Survey and remains in the top third of UK Universities (THES 2016b), but has removed much of the locally-based support originally considered essential. For the UHI "86% of students were 'quite' or 'very satisfied' with teaching that used ICT, compared with 93% for 'traditional' methods. Expectation played a role" (Panciroli et al. 2015, p. 41).

MOOCs are also having a major impact. UoL, in partnership with Coursera since 2013, had over one million enrolments on 21 MOOCs delivered from 2014–16. They then tracked over 600 MOOC students who had gone on to register on UOL International Programmes. Financially, this was very beneficial to the University. The start-up costs for their MOOCs averaged about £40,000 for a 5–6 week MOOC, while 600 full-time enrolments for three years provided about £3 million. Overall it was calculated that this provided an income of about £880,000 pa (Kerrison 2016).

If this conversion rate from MOOC learner to registered student is replicated across other HEIs who provide MOOCs, the future of HE ODeL in the UK looks promising. The OU-led *FutureLearn*, a partnership between many HEIs, had nearly 6.3 million learners by 2017, and over two million have signed up to the University of Edinburgh's MOOCs. But how far do informal learners want to sign up to fully paid-up formal programmes.

The availability of Open Educational Resources (OERs) is also having an impact. The OU's *Youtube* provides a wide range of videos and broadcasts for free; *Open-Learn* offers free uncertificated online learning which has reached over 23 million people. These informal learning opportunities provide examples of further challenges and opportunities for the future. Can informal learning at HE level be recognised and accredited within the formal structures of UK HE? Will enough students learning informally convert to registered students and so provide an economic model for the future?

Conclusion

Over 150 years, the reputation of ODeL has moved from a minor and a rather suspect form of study to a major and well accepted mode of learning. UoL External Study (now International Programmes) and the OU pioneered successful distance study, and their impact has been substantial. The OU in particular demonstrated openly how it was possible to maintain high quality teaching and learning and provide better learner support than was available at the time at some conventional universities.

Evidence for the increased recognition of ODeL study can be seen in some key areas:

- Integration within the HE sector: all current legislation in the UK treats accredited programmes in online and distance education in the same way as any other HE provision. Quality Assurance for online distance education, for example, is the same as for all other HEIs.
- Academic Quality: the open availability of all the OU's teaching materials from its first course presentation, when all other UK University teaching was (in effect) behind closed doors, could be said to have provided other Universities with benchmarks for teaching and learning.
- Student satisfaction: the OU was one of the most highly ranked Universities in the UK for "general student satisfaction" for many years after the inception of the UK NSS in 2005. By 2016, after which when many questions changed, the OU had dropped to 35th out of 160, but this remains a high rating for ODeL (THES 2016b). The tables also now include specialist medical and other Institutes which mainly cater for low numbers of postgraduate students, and so do not reflect satisfaction levels with large undergraduate providers.
- Student Employability: distance and online qualifications gained from the OU are generally regarded as good as (or sometime better than) conventional study.

Indeed some employers prefer students who have studied online or at a distance. A multinational IT and management consultancy particularly valued the ability of OU students to work at a distance: "So having the ability to think about planning things remotely, working with people who are not perhaps based in the same office, that can be a really useful skill to have…people who have genuinely thought about their career… and look for a career change, that really shows good focus, good motivation and they're the kind of people that we're looking for" (Intranet page on the OU UK's Careers Website).

A number of factors have had a major impact on the development of ODeL in the UK. Many of these are, or were, politically motivated. UoL's distance degree programmes may originally have had an imperial element but many other people, including women and Nelson Mandela, benefitted. The social justice commitment of the UK's Labour government in the 1960s to open up higher education to all led to the foundation of the Open University.

A commitment to imperial mission, social justice, regional/national autonomy and (of course) economic advantage have all played their part in the development of ODeL in the UK and governmental funding and regulatory agencies have had a major impact on developments. The effect of these has varied. However, there remains great enthusiasm at institutional and student level for increasing flexibility in teaching and learner support. The challenge is to meet student expectations within government funding, institutional constraints and a pedagogically appropriate framework for teaching and learning at a distance.

References

Ashby, A., Richardson, J. T. E., & Woodley, A. (2011). National student feedback surveys in distance education: an investigation at the UK Open University. *Open Learning: The Journal of Open, Distance and e-Learning, 26*(1), 5–25.

HESA. (2013). *Table T3e—Non-continuation two years following year of entry: UK domiciled part-time first degree entrants 2011/12.* Retrieved from https://www.hesa.ac.uk/pis/noncon.

HESA. (2016). *Statistical first release: Higher education student enrolments and qualifications obtained at higher education providers in the United Kingdom* 2014/15, SFR 224. Retrieved from https://www.hesa.ac.uk/news/14-01-2016/sfr224-enrolments-and-qualifications.

House of Commons Education and Skills Committee. (2005). *UK e-University.* Retrieved from http://www.publications.parliament.uk/pa/cm200405/cmselect/cmeduski/205/205.pdf.

Kenyon Jones, C. (2008). *The People's University 1858–2008: 150 years of the University of London and its External Students.* Cambridge University Press, University of London.

Kerrison, M. (2016). *From Present to Future of the MOOC.* Presentation at the University of London International Programmes, Centre for Distance Education Conference, 11 March 2016.

Mills, R. (1999). Diversity, convergence and the evolution of student support in higher education in the UK. In A. Tait & R. Mills (Eds.), *The convergence of distance and conventional education* (pp. 71–85). London: Routledge.

Panciroli, E., Engstrand, S., Graham, E., & Clarke, S. (2015). 'Blended' learning at the university of the highlands and islands: A case study in self-awareness and policy making. *Journal of Perspectives in Applied Academic Practice, 3*(1), 39–48. Retrieved from http://jpaap.napier.ac.uk/index.php/JPAAP/article/view/149/pdf.

QAA Quality Assurance Agency for UK Higher Education. (2010). *Code of practice for the assurance of academic quality and standards in higher education: Collaborative provision and flexible and distributed learning (including e-learning).* QAA, London, UK (*Code of practice for the assurance of academic*—Amplified version October).

QAA Quality Assurance Agency for UK Higher Education. (2012). *The quality code for UK higher education.* Retrieved from http://www.qaa.ac.uk/en/Publications/Documents/Quality-Code-introduction.pdf.

QAA Quality Assurance Agency for UK Higher Education. (2014). *Statement on massive open online courses.* Retrieved from http://www.qaa.ac.uk/en/Publications/Documents/QAA-position-statement-MOOCs.pdf.

QAA Quality Assurance Agency for UK Higher Education. (2016). *Higher education review.* Retrieved from http://www.qaa.ac.uk/reviews-and-reports/how-we-review-higher-education/higher-education-review.

Scottish Funding Council (SFC). (2017–18). *Outcome agreements for universities—Indicative funding decisions for AY 2017–18.* Retrieved from http://www.sfc.ac.uk/web/FILES/Announcements_SFCAN092017/SFC_AN_09_2017_Outcome_Agreement_Funding_for_Universities_-_Final_Allocations_for_AY_2017-18.pdf.

Simpson, O. (2004). The impact on retention of interventions to support distance learning students. *Open Learning: the Journal of Open, Distance and e-Learning, 19*(1), 79–95.

Smith, M., & Macdonald, D. (2015). Assessing quality and effectiveness in fully online distance education. *Journal of Perspectives in Applied Academic Practice 3*(1), 24–38. Retrieved from http://jpaap.napier.ac.uk/index.php/JPAAP/article/view/147.

Tait, A. (2008). What are open universities for? *Open Learning, The Journal of Open, Distance and e-Learning, 23*(2), 85–94.

Tait, A. (2016). *The end of distance education?* In Presentation at the University of London International Programmes, Centre for Distance Education Conference, March 11, 2016.

Tait, A., & Mills, R. (1999). *The convergence of distance and conventional education.* London and New York: Routledge.

The Guardian. (2017). *Part-time student numbers collapse.* Retrieved from https://www.theguardian.com/education/2017/may/02/part-time-student-numbers-collapse-universities.

THES. (2016a, March 3). *Open University posts £7 m loss as student numbers slump.* Retrieved from https://www.timeshighereducation.com/news/open-university-posts-ps7m-loss-student-numbers-slump.

THES. (2016b, August 10). *National student survey 2016: Overall satisfaction results.* Retrieved from https://www.timeshighereducation.com/student/news/national-student-survey-2016-overall-satisfaction-results.

Weinbren, D. (2015). *The open university: A history.* Manchester University in association with the Open University.

White, D., Warren.N, Faughnan, S., & Manton, M. (2010). *Study of UK online learning.* Report to HEFCE. Department for Continuing Education, University of Oxford. Retrieved from http://www.hefce.ac.uk/media/hefce/content/pubs/2010/rd1710/rd17_10.pdf.

United Kingdom—Commentary

Alan Tait

I am grateful for the opportunity to add a commentary to Anne Gaskell's very effective summary account of open, distance and e-learning in the UK. First of all, looking backwards so to speak, it is remarkable what a significant contribution major UK theorists have made to this field. The UK can claim Michael Moore, who was born and educated in the UK, and who worked at the Open University until his departure for Pennsylvania State University, whose seminal theory of transactional distance from 1971 is still cited. Similarly, the then Brit Tony Bates spent the first half of his career at the Open University where he invented the field of media and distance education, before leaving for British Columbia. We can also add Greville Rumble, who was the first scholar to examine the economics of distance education, and John Daniel, who like Moore and Bates was born and educated in the UK and spent more than a decade in leadership of the Open University. Daniel was the first to identify the crucial poles of interaction and independence in student behaviours, and went on to name and examine the phenomenon of the mega-universities. And no picture of distance education in the UK would be complete without recognition of the activist Michael Young, who invented the term 'open university' in 1962, and who set up the National Extension College which pioneered innovative practices that were influential on Open Universities everywhere. And still today the UK is producing major theorists in open education such as Martin Weller, and in learning analytics Bart Rientjes, both based at the Open University (the latter Dutch by nationality, it must be conceded). So the UK has made and continues to make a significant contribution to foundational thinking and practice, far above its size and significance in the world.

A. Tait (✉)
Emeritus of Distance Education and Development, The Open University, Milton Keynes, UK
e-mail: alan.tait@open.ac.uk

© The Author(s) 2018   99
A. Qayyum and O. Zawacki-Richter (eds.), *Open and Distance Education in Australia,*
Europe and the Americas. SpringerBriefs in Open and Distance Education,
https://doi.org/10.1007/978-981-13-0298-5_11

In terms of institutional development, as Anne Gaskell observes, the Open University as a model has been hugely influential. The development of single mode distance teaching universities around the world would not have taken place without the UK Open University to look to. Whether that has been simply the positive thing that it was thought to be by international funding organisations and national governments elsewhere is now much more open to question. So I would add a more cautionary note about this success story, as I would suggest in retrospect that the spread of the Open University model through the 1970's–1990's like many knowledge transfer processes did not take account of the social and cultural factors that made it successful in the UK In reality, although not yet honestly or openly yet acknowledged it proved to be more challenging in other countries where other models for providing large scale higher educators might have been preferable. The record of quality and student achievement in many open universities is not in truth what their founders hoped for, and it seems difficult to know how to turn this around at this stage with lack of public respect linked to poor management and funding problems. It would equally be possible to make a critique in Europe where a number of Open Universities have gone backwards or never really taken off, as well as in poorer countries. So the Open University as a global ed tech solution to scale, access and quality, which was thought to be the singular contribution of the Open University UK, can IN FACT be much more critically assessed than in former decades.

If I turn to the future I think the UK, by no means uniquely, is seeing the stability of the terminology and the field of action of open, distance and e-learning being undermined. After more than 20 years of the digital revolution technology on the campus is beginning to offer both flexibility—the core offer of ODL—and pedagogic innovation with technology enhanced learning. All campuses, more or less, have learning management systems with elements, some very sophisticated, of the curriculum available digitally, videoed lectures online for recall, assignments submitted and returned online, and email communication with the lecturer the norm. MOOCs are being studied by campus based students. Secondly, open education with its multiple dimensions of open data, open publishing, open access of libraries, open educational resources, MOOCs, and so on is by no means the province only or even primarily of the Open University, or of programmes of Open and Distance Learning. So, the very terminology of distance and e-learning may be in process of being replaced by technology enhanced learning and by open education. The challenge in some ways remains as it always has been: how to provide post-secondary education at scale with quality at a price that is affordable, and with the flexibility to permit people to come in and out during their lifetimes. The challenges of the digital revolution are reshaping provision in ways however that may make the distinctiveness of the field of distance education no longer tenable.

United States of America

Michael Beaudoin

Nearly 50 years ago, Schon (1971) urged universities to become aware of life 'beyond the stable state' and Toffler (1970) predicted that the information age would force academia to accommodate an 'accelerating pace of change.' Their prescient observations about the future have characterized American higher education for nearly 50 years, perhaps best exemplified by the role distance education (DE) has played in this process. DE's remarkable progression in the US arena began well before the electronic era, extending over a 225-year period. It is a phenomenon that perhaps represents the most significant transformation within academe in a millennium, presenting exciting opportunities and formidable challenges. This chapter offers a descriptive analysis and commentary of key aspects of DE at the post-secondary level in the US, with perspectives gained from the author's 35 years of scholarship and practice in the field.

Origins

Caleb Phillips can be credited as the 'father' of distance education in the US, who in 1728, advertised in the *Boston Gazette* that any persons in the country desirous of learning shorthand could be sent weekly lessons via the postal service, and be as well instructed as those living in Boston. Anna Tucker, founder of the Boston-based Society to Encourage Study at Home (1873–1897), might be considered the 'mother' of American correspondence education. In 1883, Illinois Wesleyan College founded the Correspondence University, and use of DE for occupation-related training occurred in Pennsylvania, evolving into International Correspondence

M. Beaudoin (✉)
University of New England, Biddeford, Maine, USA
e-mail: mbeaudoin@une.edu

© The Author(s) 2018
A. Qayyum and O. Zawacki-Richter (eds.), *Open and Distance Education in Australia, Europe and the Americas.* SpringerBriefs in Open and Distance Education,
https://doi.org/10.1007/978-981-13-0298-5_12

Schools. The first actual DE program originated with the extension division of the University of Chicago in 1892 under the leadership of William Rainey Harper (Holmberg 1995). Holmberg notes that from these beginnings, until around 1970, expansion of DE occurred with modest enhancements in delivery modes. The founding of the British Open University in 1969 brought recognition and legitimacy to the field, generating new initiatives in the US and elsewhere.

   Among influential "early adopters" of DE was the University of Wisconsin's Extension Division which, through the pioneering leadership of its director Charles Wedemeyer from the mid-50s to mid-60s, defined DE as a distinct form of educational practice. The development and implementation of DE became more acceptable as students' needs became more apparent, faculty recognized its effectiveness, and institutions became more proficient in DE design and delivery (Granger 1990). Adoption of DE was slowest in the northeastern US, home to many elite institutions reluctant to alter their centuries-old ways of educating young men from established families. Eventually, DE became a nationwide phenomenon in meeting the needs of residents dispersed over geographical expanses, especially in rural states (e.g., Maine). Common institutional models that emerged included autonomous DE mode only, and dual mode (classroom and DE). New entities (e.g., Western Governors' University) were launched, as some DE advocates recognized that transforming existing institutions to incorporate DE was not a viable option.

   It is useful to identify successive 'generations' of DE technologies:

- 1st (1950s–1960s): Single one-way modality (radio, print, TV), highly structured, delivered materials supported by instructor;
- 2nd (1960–85): Multiple modes (audio-video cassettes, TV, print, fax), prepackaged, structured materials for independent study;
- 3rd (1985–95): Multiple modes (computers and networking using broadband enabling 2-way communication (email, audioconference, chat, satellite, cable, phone, print), structured materials able to accommodate interactive technologies providing direction and support to learners;
- 4th (1995–2005): Multiple technologies (email, chat, computer networks, Internet, high bandwidth transmission enabling individualized, customized, live interactive exchanges, satellite, video and audioconferencing, phone, fax);
- 5th (2005–15): Multiple technologies and applications similar to 3rd and 4th generation; mass ownership of computers and online support services; increased attention to instructional design; more open access to resources (Boettcher and Foster 1996).

US-based DE was initially sponsored primarily by public 4-year universities, followed by for-profit entities, and eventually by private institutions and many 2-year community colleges, thereby encompassing the entire gamut of higher education offering hundreds of degree programs characterized by diverse delivery modes. This pattern emulated the earlier proliferation of private liberal arts colleges, rise of public land grant universities, expansion of community colleges, and creation of the GI Bill for post-WW11 veterans-all notable events affecting generations of students in the US. Clearly, the Internet/WWW have had the most profound effect on US higher education in the current era. The US environment never fostered the phenomenon of mega-universities with tens of thousands of enrollments as was the case in other countries (e.g., Thailand, China, Korea). It was not until 1996 that the first major 'from the ground up' online institution (University of Phoenix) was founded. It began offering classroom-based instruction in non-campus venues, then instituted an online delivery system that grew exponentially, eventually becoming the largest online institution in the US.

Miller (2011) described the simultaneous diversification and convergence of technologies that advanced DE. In the 1980's, technologies available for instruction were relatively few and simple; a decade later technology had changed dramatically in that it didn't just reach individual students, but extended the traditional classroom environment to all The creation of two-way interaction between teacher and students, and students with fellow students advanced the effectiveness of DE, enabling exchanges among communities of students across time and space. Miller notes that this technology-rich environment had important implications beyond course design and delivery; it changed the way we define DE (i.e., not by the technology used, but rather by the nature of interaction involved in the educational process).

The creation of national professional entities to support DE-related activities was a long time in coming. Early efforts focused on correspondence study, later followed by a broader view of practice labeled 'distance education,' terminology formally adopted in 1982 with the creation of the International Council of Distance Education. As instructional technology went from being novel to ubiquitous, it fostered the establishment of organizations to support individual and institutional users (e.g., National University Teleconference Network). Funding sources identified DE as a worthwhile initiative for support (e.g., Annenberg/CPB Project, beginning in 1981), mainly for design of courses utilizing media.

In the earlier years of DE's development in the US, no national body, governmental or private, materialized to serve as a centralized coordinating entity to promote, oversee, and assess DE planning and policy. As late as 1990, Hezel maintained that policy formulation remained a relatively low priority among most DE providers, and that few state or local projects had written or published a coherent set of policies to guide their planning and practices. The annual US Congress Office of Technology Assessment Report now offers federal and state policy recommendations for DE planners, with emphasis on policies relating to governance, management, planning, finances, communication, and accreditation. Gradually, various nationally-oriented groups contributed to these growing endeavors [e.g., the American Council on Education promulgated 'guiding principles' for DE (1996)].

Despite relatively little collaboration among hundreds of US institutions that have developed a vast array of DE offerings utilizing different delivery systems, most adopted some version of Peters' so-called industrialized approach to course production (Peters, in Keegan 1993). Though most faculty accustomed to the guild tradition of developing and teaching their own courses as their exclusive intellectual property resisted the team approach, it has become accepted practice by most DE providers. Long-held practices (e.g., copyright law, fair usage), underwent modifications through the presence of DE. DE became acceptable at many institutions not necessarily because they embraced the concept, but rather because it was seen as a revenue-producing function that met the increasing expectation of on-demand access to higher education.

Impact on Higher Education

Has a 'paradigm shift' in US higher education occurred as a consequence of DE? Have integrated digital technologies encouraged a rethinking of the role of higher education, something the academy has long resisted? Some critics, taking the broad view of DE, allege that we have witnessed the massive deployment of 21st century technology, yet the result has been to essentially reinvent the 18th century university on a more global scale (Conley 2010). Technology-assisted learning has not displaced face-to-face pedagogy in the US as some faculty feared, but has produced changes that have moved the campus-centric model closer to a consumer-centric one. Academe's reaction to DE has largely been dictated by perceptions of it as either opportunity or threat. Correspondence courses represented a relatively benign alternative to classroom instruction, and so encountered less opposition than did the introduction of the online format which threatened conventional teaching and its teachers.

The early evolution of DE and its adoption by more institutions contributed to what might be called the 'institutionalization' of DE in the US, changing its image from a cottage industry to a growing segment of higher education at a pace sustained over at least the past two decades and which only recently shows any sign of abetting (Allen and Seaman 2013, 2014). Though the dramatic growth of DE expanded access to higher education, doubling and diversifying the post-secondary student population, a provocative question regarding the higher education landscape prevails: Despite the appearance of innovation, has DE largely occurred within the accepted paradigms of academe with scant evidence of fundamental change?

As so-called 'virtual' universities emerged (e.g., Western Governors' University), more options became available to learners. Although the residential college remained largely intact, electronic campuses emerged to provide flexible 'anytime-anyplace' learning integrating classroom and electronic components, and increasing continuing professional education and training augmented by employers and non-academic organizations. New technologies and shifting demographics placed new demands on institutions adopting DE, requiring new infrastructure and systems to meet the differing lifestyles and expectations of learners. A common institutional conundrum has been whether to create a central unit to coordinate all DE activities, or to allow each sponsoring unit to manage its own.

The changing landscape forced added attention to areas such as student services and course schedules, which many institutions had taken for granted, assuming that prevailing means of doing business could remain intact regardless of new trends. But diminishing resources and increasing enrollments demanded greater productivity, economies of scale, focus on quality, and attention to competition-aspects that many institutions did not possess expertise needed to respond in an orderly, timely fashion. These challenges could not be ignored, and were exacerbated by new student markets choosing educational providers on the basis of convenience and price rather than geography and prestige. These realities prompted many institutions to reinvent themselves, creating new entities to better respond, or integrating new elements into existing modalities, attempting to reduce costs without sacrificing quality or reputation. Those that resisted change, preferring to rely on traditional modes and markets for continued success, did so at their own peril, and as enrollments declined, some did not survive.

One example of a struggling institution that morphed into a leading online provider is University of Southern New Hampshire, largely propelled by a president with online education expertise and a commitment to consumer needs. It began its online offerings in 1995 and currently enrolls 34,000 DE students, with 5 off-campus sites, over 200 undergraduate and graduate degree programs, many customized to serve domestic, international, and military learners.

Any change is likely to cause discontinuity with prevailing practice, what Christensen (1997) refers to as disruptive technology, and though it may spawn innovation, it does not come about easily. The evolution of DE in American higher education reflects this disruptive element that persists in many settings to the present, as evidenced by faculty skepticism, tensions between traditional values and new practices, and competition for limited resources. This phenomenon is accentuated by new technology requiring constant adaptation to incorporate the latest features, just when providers and users become comfortable using the last innovation, causing further disruption. This technological transience has been a reality of DE in the US for at least the past two decades. Yet, it is important to recognize that DE has survived and ultimately thrived within the US landscape, a testimonial to those pioneers committed to pursuing this goal, often when the climate surrounding them offered little support. Though the conventional classroom remains at the epicenter of pedagogy, technology-supported learning management systems are a dominant DE feature that represents a digital *tsunami*.

A key question is whether DE has reached a "Tipping Point" in the US or elsewhere. If so, what is the evidence for this, and if not, when will it occur? When online enrollments exceed classroom enrollments? When students and faculty choose online courses as their preferred option for learning and teaching? When institutions reward faculty for accomplishments in the online milieu? When distinctions between face-to-face and online instruction are blurred? When electronic global 'campuses' are commonplace? Despite impressive gains in DE that meet some of these criteria, it clearly has not yet supplanted mainstream higher education in the US. Indeed, conflicting opinions persist among faculty, employers, and learners regarding the merits of online learning.

Enrollment Growth

Innumerable surveys have been conducted to chronicle DE growth in the US, particularly in the online era. By the mid-1980s, 65 US institutions offered degrees through DE (Perry 1984) at a time when relatively few European institutions did so. Findings of the National Survey of Desktop Computing in Higher Education (1996) indicate that by the mid-1990s, IT usage grew dramatically (e.g., the percentage of college courses using electronic and multi-media resources between 1994 and 1995 more than doubled).Other survey results: An estimated 753, 640 students formally enrolled in DE courses; one-third of all institutions offered DE courses; 62% of public 4-year institutions offered DE courses compared with 12% of private institutions doing so; and a quarter of institutions offered degrees that could be completed through DE courses exclusively.

Approximately 2,876,000 students enrolled in DE courses in 2000, a nearly 100% increase since 1997; 56% of 2 and 4-year institutions offered DE courses in 2001–2; 90% offered by public institutions (National Center for Educational Statistics NCES 2004). Noteworthy is that public institutions provided nearly twice as many online courses as private institutions. By 2003, online enrollments were growing 20% annually; much of this growth occurred in the for-profit sector, which accounted for 2/5ths of the $5 billion in higher education revenues (NCES 2004).

In the 2000s, enrollment in all (4100+) post-secondary institutions increased from 16.9 million to 20.4 million, including online enrollments of 46% in public institutions and 42% in for-profit colleges (EDVENTURES, *The Chronicle of Higher Education* 2010). In 2010, University of Phoenix had the largest online enrollments (380,000), equaling combined enrollments of the next 9 largest online institutions (US News and World Report-Education 2010). In 2012, 5.3 million online enrollments reflected a 3.7% increase, but an 8.7% decrease in for-profit numbers) (Babson 2013), with half in fully online programs. Among 1300 academic and business leaders surveyed by Pew (2011), 57% agreed that in 10 years, a majority of students would obtain part of their education via virtual classes.

In fall 2013, 5,522,192 students were enrolled in DE courses (NCES 2016). The latest Babson report indicated a 3.9% one-year increase in DE students, to 5.8 million, with approximately half taking all of their courses at a distance. Public institutions continued to represent a significantly larger proportion of DE students. Despite these impressive numbers, the percentage of chief academic officers who say online learning is critical to their long- term strategy fell from 71 to 63%, and only 29% report their faculty accepts the "value and legitimacy of online education." Schools with the largest DE enrollments report 60% faculty acceptance, while 11.6% of faculty at schools with no DE do so (Babson 2015).

Among the factors that have fostered recent growth in US online enrollments has been the lifting of the so-called "50% rule", legislation the US Congress passed in 1992 to counter the proliferation of 'diploma mills' and correspondence programs that began in the 1980s. The regulation prevented any college that enrolled more than 50% of its students or provided more than 50% of its courses at a distance from participating in federal student-aid programs. Despite concern that a change would prompt an online boom and create more diploma mills, the restriction ended in 2006, but remained in effect for correspondence programs. Those endorsing the demise of the rule argued that (1) it discouraged institutions from launching new initiatives that better serve nontraditional students, and (2) it was unnecessary because state and regional accrediting agencies do an adequate job of preventing fraud and inferior programs from continued operation.

In mid-2016 the U.S. Department of Education (DOE) proposed regulations to improve oversight of DE programs by clarifying state requirements for institutions to participate in federal student aid programs. A longstanding requirement is that institutions be authorized in the state in which they are located for eligibility to receive federal student aid. While institutions must have authorization in the states in which they are physically located, there are no federal requirements for DE providers in states where they are not physically located. The proposed regulations close this loophole, alarming some state regulators because it would lead to an influx of institutions they need to review (www.ed.gov/news/press-releases/education, (July 22, 2016).

Role of Faculty

A primary reason why DE did not become more readily amalgamated with conventional teaching on US campuses has been due to intractable faculty resistance. Other impediments include the absence of viable infrastructure to facilitate IT, and the lack of effective leadership to advance DE. Also, early IT interest among faculty was often focused on acquiring new tools for research rather than applying them to their pedagogy. Most faculty used IT primarily for email, word processing, Web searches, and finding materials to augment their face-to-face courses. When teaching issues were addressed, it was often in the context of how to adapt new technology to old pedagogy.

Though new technologies enabled enhanced pedagogy, skeptical instructors were reluctant to take advantage of these resources. They did not know what was relatively easy to do using IT; they were not especially interested in IT if it did not facilitate their research; IT changed too rapidly and was seen as disruptive; they did not feel their institution spent adequate funds on technology; they believed technology would encumber their teaching rather than enrich it (Allitt 2005). At the other end of the continuum were teachers whose over-reliance on technology sent the message that machines are necessary for students to learn, while lessening the need for teachers to actually teach. But as course management systems proliferated and more features were offered, users' expectations rose, and more teachers and students depended on them. Instructors' primary role shifted from providing content to facilitating the learning process (Beaudoin 1990).

A conspicuous lacuna among many teacher-education programs was the absence of guidance in how to incorporate technology into pedagogy. This weakness is later exacerbated if institutions provide minimal training to new faculty employed to teach online. Despite increased attention to this, a Babson College survey (2010) of training for online teaching reported that 5.6% received no training, and 57% received only informal mentoring. Another Babson survey (2008–9) found that only 12–13% of faculty rated their institution above average in providing incentives and recognition for developing and delivering online courses. A probable consequence of this is that only 28% of all faculty accepts the value and legitimacy of online education (Babson 2013).

The Digital Age has introduced a new paradigm into the teaching-learning equation: Web-centric courses, high interactivity, varying formats, resources accessed via computer networks, greater student independence in managing learning. These developments have brought faculty-related issues to the fore, including: promotion and tenure, release time, course load, curriculum revision, publishing, compensation, and intellectual property- all areas of faculty life that had remained largely unchanged for decades. Pervasive resistance from much of the professoriate persists, so much so that Ayers (2005) maintains the fundamental principles of academe remain largely unchanged because of conflicting priorities (e.g., the academy values physical place and stability; DE emphasizes mobility and change).

Online Learning as a Strategic Asset

As DE gravitated from the fringes of higher education, it finally became recognized as a strategic institutional asset. Findings based on 231 interviews with administrators, faculty and students at 45 public institutions and 11,000 survey responses from faculty (McCarthy and Samors 2009) illustrate this development. Online learning programs:

– work effectively as a core component of strategic planning and implementation;
– benefit from ongoing institutional assessment and review;
– are strengthened by centralization of key functions;
– may be more readily accepted if overseen by academic units;
– need reliable financing mechanisms for sustainability and growth;
– succeed with adequate resources for faculty and students;
– have the capacity to change campus culture if campus leaders communicate that DE is fundamental to the institution's mission and priorities.

A striking findings is that although more than two-thirds of responding CEOs recognize that online programs are strategically important to their institution, less than one-half actually included online programs in their strategic plans. This, despite the number of students taking online courses continues to expand at a rate far in excess of overall enrollments (Ibid.).

For-Profit Providers, Partnerships, and Economics

Higher education is a significant industry in the US economy. The total average cost for one year of college is $20,400, and some charge $60,000 or more annually (NCES 2016). For-profit DE institutions have played a significant role in the US market. Most such entities have been recognized as efficient, innovative, and engaged in improving quality in their offerings. Flexible scheduling, relevant programs, robust student services, and effective recruiting have enabled many to rapidly expand and become highly profitable. Yet success has invited scrutiny, particularly from the US Department of Education (DOE), citing high attrition, excessive course enrollments, lack of rigor compared to classroom instruction, and claims that employers are hesitant to employ graduates of online degree programs. These aspects are viewed as indications of failure, while administrators of proprietary programs argue these are among the myths DE programs must overcome. DOE now more actively exercises its regulatory authority, especially regarding financial aid practices, but in most matters, it largely defers to states' monitoring and authorization.

Many institutions charge a premium for online courses, and some add a surcharge for hybrid courses. A survey by Campus Computing Project/WCET (Parry 2010) found that among 182 institutions, nearly half charged more for online than classroom courses. Those charging less for online instruction are often criticized by online faculty who feel this conveys that such courses are 'not as good' as campus-based offerings, and thus provides ammunition to skeptics. Further, cheaper online courses can undercut classroom course numbers. Online courses have obviously made education more accessible and convenient (for providers and consumers), but not necessarily more economical, even in an era when institutions attempt to achieve economies of scale to reduce costs while maintaining standards.

Despite academes inherent parochialism, expansion-oriented institutions have recognized the benefits of establishing formal collaborations, typically in the form of consortia with like-minded counterparts, or partnerships with for-profit organizations. These arrangements have generally been quite successful, though certainly some have resulted in more conflict than collaboration, as differing goals a may clash. This is especially so when international collaborations are attempted in unfamiliar cultural milieus. Nonetheless, many successful DE enterprises among US institutions would not have thrived without the advantages of a corporate partnership providing expertise in non-academic functions, such as marketing, recruiting, technical support, and student services (e.g., University of New England-USA launched several DE programs from 'scratch' in the early 90s utilizing corporate partners; currently, without need for these alliances, 1/3rd of its offerings are online). It is assumed that these 'opportunistic alliances' are more cost-effective than offering DE unilaterally, yet there is no clear evidence to support this belief (Hough 1992). But there are typical advantages including: reduced costs, less duplication, higher quality courses, enhanced services, and expanded options for learners.

Accreditation and Quality Assurance

As DE programs were added to the portfolio of more institutions, US providers were understandably concerned about how accrediting bodies would assess them, fearing they might be held to different or higher standards than conventional programs. But generally, similar criteria have been crafted by the 6 regional agencies and so have not constrained DE initiatives. For example, the New England accrediting body established DE policies in 1998; these did not replace its Standards for Accreditation, but rather specified ways its standards are applicable to DE programs, and provided examples of evidence. Eventually, with adoption of guidelines developed by the Western Interstate Commission on Higher Education, quality control in DE expanded from regional to national cooperation (Lezberg 2007). Quality Matters, an international organization that assists with ensuring high standards in online course design and delivery is a widely used resource. The Distance Education Training Council serves as a national accrediting group (mainly reviewing proprietary programs), augmenting periodic peer-reviewed assessments conducted by regional accrediting agencies. Twigg (2010) observed that lingering concern remains about the quality of online education, even among accredited institutions, despite the fact that all are subject to quality assurance systems, and the distinction between DE and face-to-face modes is blurring.

Social and Ethical Issues

The impact of computers on education providers and consumers in the US, as elsewhere, has been enormous. This phenomenon has affected the American professoriate as well as students immersed in a virtual world powered by online tools (and toys). These resources offer users enhanced experiences in many activities and endeavors, but there can be a 'dark side' to this realm. As Turkle (2011) has chronicled, the current digital generation often has difficulty distinguishing reality versus simulations of it. Turkle (2004) is alarmed that the virtual environments self-directed learners constantly inhabit compromise the quality of their social and educational interaction. She offers evidence that as students become more adept at instant word processing, it is often at the expense of deep thinking and effective use of language. Another issue is that learners' access to multiple sources of information requires choices about what material is most relevant and reliable, a skill inexperienced researchers lack. As more educational providers make courseware accessible mainly via online sources, and require students to function exclusively in online settings, it becomes an all-consuming lifestyle. The ethical implications of this are unavoidable.

The pervasive impact of technology has heightened attention to appropriate ethical behaviors expected of students by those who plan, manage and evaluate DE activities, but are providers as attentive to their own practices? Much effort is made to encourage or enforce guidelines for students to adhere to in their online learnings, but this may be less so for instructors. This is not to suggest that inappropriate behavior is noticeably present in the US professoriate, but rather to note that the digital revolution in academe can create situations in which individuals and organizations may overlook or ignore areas in which ethical practice could be compromised. The dissemination and enforcement of ethical standards for DE practice in the US have not been actively undertaken by local or federal governments. It has been largely left to the discretion of institutional providers to articulate their own expectations, though accrediting agencies and many professional associations do identify areas of preferred behavior among their constituencies.

Consideration of ethics in DE usually elicits opinions regarding the issue of equity in terms of access and opportunity for learning. Many DE advocates envisioned that the availability of virtual resources would shrink the so-called digital divide and thus 'democratize' higher education worldwide. The US would seem to possess ideal conditions to be especially effective in this transformation compared to many resource-impoverished nations. Ironically, despite its technological advances, socio-economic disparities in the knowledge-based society have persisted, and while online enrollments have swelled, tuition costs have risen so dramatically that many are still denied opportunities for further education. Community colleges are notable exceptions in this regard, and exponential growth at some of these institutions reflect this commitment.

The Future

The dramatic changes in the learning landscape fostered by DE over the past several decades have prompted theorists and practitioners to prognosticate about the future, within the current decade and beyond. DE is currently characterized by many of its converts as the exemplar of how teaching and learning should occur. But, we might soon view DE, as we now know it, to be outmoded when supplanted by new tools currently beyond our comprehension. American academics have a penchant for assuming most educational innovation originated in the US, and will have a lasting worldwide impact. The US, in DE as well as other sectors, pioneered major theories and practices currently in vogue, but some trends can move in reverse. For example, MOOCS (massive open online courses) and collaborative learning facilitated by social media and other interactive tools are dominant features of DE, enabling hundreds, even thousands of learners to share a common educational experience. Yet, MOOCs have already lost some currency, and Moore recently editorialized that, despite its virtues, online group interdependence can occur at the expense of autonomous learning (Moore 2015). In a subsequent editorial Moore (2016) enthuses about greater emphasis on 'personalized learning' and how emerging trends encourage new innovative approaches to DE pedagogy.

It is interesting to consider what a group of practitioners convening in 1996 to imagine the future university prognosticated what the learning environment might look like 10 years later: Fewer institutions; more differentiation among them; more for-profit educational enterprises; the end of geographic hegemony; more educational brokers functioning as credit banks and credentialing services; and increasing demand for higher education worldwide. The group cautioned that higher education would have to anticipate and address these new realities if they wished to succeed. Yet, overriding their deliberations about the future was the fundamental question of whether or not this sector has the capacity to change in order to accommodate and thrive, or indeed, to survive a prospective new educational world order? (Twigg and Oblinger 1996).

Many of these phenomena have since been realized in the US and elsewhere. Yet, it cannot be ignored that DE, despite its remarkable advances, still remains as somewhat of an anomaly on many campuses, and its practices, including large-scale enterprises (e.g., MOOCs), are still viewed as alternatives to mainstream education. Perhaps, only when leaders recognize that DE is a strategic force for institutional transformation, and when "Old Millennium" ways of doing are replaced by "New Millennium" thinking, will that elusive "tipping point" truly be achieved. It is those with vision able to articulate, advocate and operationalize these goals who will ultimately make their organizations relevant for the digital age and for all citizens in the US and beyond who now live in a complex global community.

References

Allen, E., & Seaman, J. (2013). Changing course: Ten years of tracking online education in the United States. Oakland, CA: Babson Survey Research Group. Retrieved June 28, 20016 from http://www.onlinelearningsurvey.com/reports/changingcourse.pdf.

Allen, E., & Seaman, J. (2014). Grade change—tracking online education in the United States. Oakland, CA: Babson Survey Research Group. Retrieved June 28, 2016 from http://www.onlinelearningsurvey.com/reports/gradechange.pdf.

Allitt, P. (2005, June 24). Professors, stop your microchips. *The Chronicle of Higher Education-Information Technology*, pp. B38–39.

American Council on Education. (1996). Guiding principles for distance learning in a learning society (1996). Washington, DC.

Ayers, E. (2005, November–December). Harmonizing the realms of academe and IT. *Education Review.*

Babson Survey Research Group. (2009). Strong faculty engagement in online learning. Retrieved February 22, 2016 from http://onlinelearningconsortium.org/read/survey-reports.

Babson Survey Research Group. (2010, November 5). Online learning by the numbers. *The Chronicle of Higher Education/Online Learning*, p. B28.

Babson Survey Research Group. (2013). Grade level: Tracking online education in the US. *US News & World Report-Education*. Retrieved February 22, 2016 from www.usnews.com/education.

Babson Survey Research Group. (2015). Online report card: tracking online education in the US. Retrieved July 7, 2016 from www.onlinelearningsurvey.com/highered.html.

Beaudoin, M. (1990). The instructor's changing role in distance education. *The American Journal of Distance Education 4*(2), 21–29 (University Park, PA: The Pennsylvania State University).

Boettcher, J. & Foster, B. (1996). Florida state university (Unpublished manuscript, adapted from A. Bates (1995) *Technology, open learning and distance education.* New York: Routledge).

Christensen, C. (1997). *The innovator's dilemma.* Boston: Harvard Business School Press.

Conley, D. (2010, November 5). Steal this education. *The Chronicle of Higher Education/Online Learning*, pp. B 39–41.

Granger, D. (1990, July/August). Open universities-closing the distances to learning. *Change*, pp. 45–50.

Hezel, R. (1990). Policies for educational technology: A national, state and local agenda. In A. Sheely (Ed.) *Educational policy and telecommunications technologies*. Washington, DC: US Department of Education.

Holmberg, B. (1995, June). The evolution of the character and practice of distance education. *Open Learning*, 47–53.

Hough, P. (1992). *The impact of distance education on the organization of schools and school systems in Alberta* (Unpublished doctoral dissertation). University of Alberta, Edmonton, Alberta.

Keegan, D. (Ed.). (1993). *Theoretical principles of distance education*. London, UK: Routledge.

Lezberg, A. (2007). Accreditation: Quality control in distance higher education. In M. Moore (Ed.). *Handbook of distance education (2nd ed.)*. Mahwah, NJ: Lawrence Erlbaum Associates, Publishers.

McCarthy, S. & Samors, R. (2009). Online learning as a strategic asset. Volume 1: A resource for campus leaders. Washington, DC: Association of Public/Land Grant Universities.

Moore, M. (1997). Theory of transactional distance. In D. Keegan (Ed.) (1997), *Theoretical principles of distance education*. London, UK: Routledge.

Moore, M. G. (2015, October–December). Editorial. *The American Journal of Distance Education* 29(4), 229–31.

Moore, M. (2016, April–June). Editorial. *The American Journal of Distance Education. 30*(2), 65–67.

Miller, G. (January 28, 2011). Long-term trends in distance education. *DEOSNEWS*, 2(23). The distance education online symposium.

National Center for Education Statistics. (2004). *The condition of education—2004*. Washington, DC. Retrieved May 20, 2016 from http://nces.ed.gov/programs.

National Center for Education Statistics. (2016). *The condition of education—2016*. Washington, DC. Retrieved July 10, 2016 from http://nces.ed.gov/programs.

Parry, M. (2010, November 5). Such a deal? Maybe not. *The Chronicle of Higher Education/Online Learning*, pp. B12–15.

Perry, W. (1984). *The state of distance learning worldwide*. Milton Keynes, UK: International Center for Distance Learning of the United Nations University.

Pew Research Center. (2011, August 19). The Digital revolution and higher education. Retrieved February 23, 2016.

Schon, D. (1971). *Beyond the stable state*. New York: Random House.

Toffler, A. (1970). *Future shock*. New York: Random House.

Turkle, S. (2004, January 30). How computers change the way we think. *The Chronicle Review-Information Technology*, pp. B26–27.

Turkle, S. (2011). *Alone together: Why we expect more from technology and less from. each other*. New York: Basic Books.

Twigg, C., & Oblinger. D. (1996, November 5–6). *The Virtual University*. Report of Joint Educom/IBM Roundtable, Washington, DC.

Twigg, C. (2010, November 5). Has the quality of online learning kept up with its growth? *The Chronicle of Higher Education/Online Learning*, p. B44.

U.S. News and World Report-Education. (2010, October 14). *10 largest online schools*. Retrieved February 23, 2016 www.usnews.com/education.

U.S. Department of Education, National Center for Education Statistics. (2016). Digest of Education Statistics, 2015 (NCES 2016-014), Table 311.15.

U.S. Department of Education. *Department proposes rule state authorization postsecondary distance education foreign institutions*. Retrieved July 31, 2016 from www.ed.gov/news/press-releases/education (July 22, 2016).

United States—Commentary

Gary E. Miller

There are more than 4700 institutions of higher education in the United States. These include technical institutes, community colleges, state colleges and universities, a landgrant university in each state, private liberal arts colleges, private research universities, and, more recently, for-profit degree-granting companies. While distance education was once primarily the purview of land grant universities and, later, community colleges, online learning has greatly broadened the diversity of institutions that provide programs to students away from campus. One factor that makes it difficult to discuss a "national system" of distance education in the United States is that higher education tends to be organized at the state level rather than nationally. At the national level, distance education innovations tend to be shared within families of institutions through their own professional associations (American Association of Community Colleges, University Professional and Continuing Education Association, etc.). One major exception is the Online Learning Consortium, which was formed when the Alfred P. Sloan Foundation brought together institutions that it had funded through its "asynchronous learning networks" grants program in the 1990s. That said, there is a long tradition of institutional collaboration that cuts across many distance education technologies and governance boundaries.

In the heyday of correspondence study, most U.S. distance education providers were land grant universities that belonged to the National University Extension Association (now called the University Professional and Continuing Education Association). For the most part, the emphasis was on courses rather than degree programs. NUEA member institutions published a unified course catalog that was widely used.

In the late 1970s, the Public Broadcasting Service (PBS) shifted its national television delivery technology to satellite. This created a nation-wide platform for

G. E. Miller (✉)
Executive Director Emeritus, Pennsylvania State University World Campus, University Park, Pennsylvania, USA
e-mail: gem7@psu.edu

© The Author(s) 2018

A. Qayyum and O. Zawacki-Richter (eds.), *Open and Distance Education in Australia, Europe and the Americas*, SpringerBriefs in Open and Distance Education, https://doi.org/10.1007/978-981-13-0298-5_13

sharing of video-based distance education courses. Courses were downloaded to local stations via satellite and then broadcast, with local institutions licensing the use of individual courses to offer credit. The PBS satellite system also fostered other kinds of collaboration. One—the National University Teleconferencing Network—allowed universities to distribute live, noncredit seminars to other higher education institutions, which would host local viewing and discussion sessions at their local stations. Another, AG*SAT (today called ADEC, the American Distance Education Consortium), networked Cooperative Extension Offices around the country, sharing research transfer information to researchers and practitioners across states. Another collaborative, the International University Consortium, adapted highly interdisciplinary course packages from the Open University of the United Kingdom to the North American curriculum and licensed their use to individual institutions.

The online environment eliminated geography as a defining factor in the institution's relationship with the student. It also shifted the emphasis from single courses to complete degree programs. Head-to-head competition for students has tended to work against some kinds of collaboration. However, it has also stimulated new collaborations. One example is the Great Plains IDEA (Interactive Distance Education Alliance), through which state universities in the American Midwest have developed collaborative degree programs to ensure that students in specialized degree programs have access to the best content from across the region, regardless of their home state. Students take online courses from multiple institutions to complete the degree. Another example is the Community College Consortium for Open Educational Resources, a collaborative of two-year colleges from 21 states that promotes policies and practices around the use of OERs to expand student access and faculty choice of materials to use in courses.

The growth of online distance education for undergraduate and graduate degree programs has been accompanied at many institutions by a decrease in traditional continuing education, especially noncredit engagements for training and research transfer. Looking ahead, there is an opportunity for institutions to use online distance education to build new inter-sector relationships with key constituencies. This might include partnerships with K-12 schools to share OERs and to offer dual-enrollment courses that improve the potential that students will graduate from high school prepared to move on to higher education. It might also include the development of online learning communities that bring together higher education institutions and industries or professional organizations to ensure that employees have access to professional development and new research results and that use social media to maintain a dialog between faculty and practitioners to solve problems and generate new research challenges.

Online distance education is gradually blurring the old distinctions among institutions, while opening new pathways for engagement with the community.

Distance Education in Australia, Europe and the Americas

Adnan Qayyum and Olaf Zawacki-Richter

Most countries discussed in this book are not new to open and distance education, but there are many new developments in open and distance education in most countries. This chapter provides an analysis of ODE in Australia, Brazil, Canada, Germany, the United Kingdom and United States, according to what the authors have written about the status and trends in ODE in their countries. In the previous chapters, many notable issues and trends emerge about changes to ODE. These include: the size of ODE enrollments; the amount that ODE enrollments constitute HE enrollments as a whole; the rate of growth in ODE enrollments; the role of the private sector in providing ODE programs; the varied use of ICTs for ODE provision; the role and influence of government policy; the opportunities and challenges for ODE providers; the digital transformation of higher education more generally; and the role of ODE in growing the acceptance of education as a private good. These are the topics of this chapter.

Size and growth of ODE

There are over 8.5 million higher education students taking a distance education course from institutions in Australia, Brazil, Canada, Germany, the United Kingdom and United States. The number of students taking ODE courses are listed in Table 1.

A. Qayyum (✉)
Pennsylvania State University, University Park, PA, USA
e-mail: adnan@psu.edu

O. Zawacki-Richter
Carl Von Ossietzky Universität Oldenburg, Oldenburg, Germany
e-mail: olaf.zawacki.richter@uni-oldenburg.de

© The Author(s) 2018   121
A. Qayyum and O. Zawacki-Richter (eds.), *Open and Distance Education in Australia,*
Europe and the Americas, SpringerBriefs in Open and Distance Education,
https://doi.org/10.1007/978-981-13-0298-5_14

Table 1 Enrollment in Open and Distance Education

Country	Enrollment in ODE courses	Higher education students taking ODE (%)
Australia	261,000	18.7
Brazil	1,341,842	17.1
Canada	361,000	29.0
Germany	154,325	5.5
United Kingdom	173,889	7.7
United States	6,359,121	31.6%

(These numbers are based on the data from the book chapters, and official government sources. ODE enrollments are not a straightforward number. Enrollments can be calculated in different ways including number of students who are fully ODE students, and number of students taking one or more ODE courses. As there is no standard for counting ODE enrollments, the data provided here is based on the figures provided by authors in the chapters. Additionally, the year for the data varies. For Australia, the data is from 2017, from 2018 for the year 2016 from US, 2015 for Canada and the UK, and 2014 for Brazil and Germany.)

The figures in the table are the minimum number of students enrolled in ODE in these countries. These numbers do not it include enrollments in Massive Open Online Courses, MOOCs. Nor do they include, in some cases, thousands of students outside of these countries enrolled in ODE courses within those countries. For example, in Australia the 261,000 enrollments represent students in the country but studying off-campus where lesson materials, assignments, etc. are delivered to students off campus and attendance on campus is usually not required. In the United Kingdom, the data is the minimum number of ODE students. It includes enrollments only from the Open University. As Gaskell states in her chapter, the OU is not the only provider of open and distance learning in the UK. It is just the most well-known. There is no current data about campus-based institutions offering ODE in the UK. However, other data suggests that many international students were studying from abroad but at UK institutions using DE. According to the Higher Education Statistics Agency in Britain (HESA 2016), there were at least 114,000 students outside the UK studying at UK institutions via DE. The majority of these offshore students were from the European Union. The OU is not among the top 20 institutions where these students were studying. Based on this dataset, we can estimate that the enrollments of ODE are probably at least 340,000. In the United States in 2016, there were 3.00 million students taking all of their courses via ODE and another 3.36 million taking some courses via ODE (Seaman et al. 2018, p. 3).

It is not just the size of the absolute number of ODE enrollments that is notable. ODE enrollments are an important part of the overall higher education enrollments. In Australia, ODE students are 18.7% of all higher education students. This number is likely over 20% if ODE enrollments are included from the private consortium, the Open University of Australia. Brazil has a similar number of ODE students at 17.1%. In Canada, nearly 30% of higher education students are taking online courses. In Germany, ODE students constitute 5.5% of all students enrolled in universities, including universities of applied science (Fachhochschulen) and the FernUniversitat. In the UK, ODE students are at least 7.7% of all university students. For the United States, 14% of all higher education students were taking all of their courses via ODE, and nearly 30% of all higher education students were taking at least one course via distance. Among the six countries, on average 17.7% of all higher education students take some or all of their courses via ODE. As the UK and Australia numbers suggest, this is likely a low calculation.

Growth of ODE

In most countries, the demand for ODE continues to grow. For nearly all countries, the authors indicate there is a growth in the absolute number and percentage of ODE enrollments from previous years. The exception here is the United Kingdom. In Australia, ODE enrollments rose four percent from 2016 to 2017. In Brazil, the overall growth rate averaged 10% per year from 2009 to 2014 for distance-based student enrollments. During the decade, the growth rate ranged from 4% for 2012 to 2013, to a 16% growth rate from 2013 to 2014. Canada has had an annual growth rate of 8.75% for the last 10 years. In Germany, ODE enrollments have been growing unevenly. Enrollments grew near or above 30% a year from 2009 to 2011. Then it grew just over 7% a year from 2011 to 2013, before falling to just 0.9% growth from 2013 to 2014. In the United States, ODE enrollments have grown at about 5.6% from 2015 to 2016 (Seaman et al. 2018, p. 12).

In the UK, there has been an overall decline in ODE enrollments. In 2009–2010 there were more than 260,000 students enrolled in the OU and by 2014–15 there were just under 174,000 students enrolled. This has led to a 7.2% annual decline in OU enrollments from 2010 to 2015. Government policy and funding changes have substantially affected higher education enrollments as a whole, including enrollments for open and distance education at the Open University and other institutions offering DE courses. After the austerity budgets of the UK government, there were less monies for public funding generally, including for higher education. A new government funding structure for higher education in 2012 increased tuition fees for students substantially. This has led to less adult learners and part-time students enrolling in higher education. These students historically have been an important body of DE enrollments.

There is a huge demand for higher education in general, and the annual growth rates understate how dramatic the growth of ODE has been in many countries. In Brazil, there were less than 50,000 students enrolled in ODE in 2003. By 2014 there were over 1.3 million students enrolled in ODE. The overall growth in ODE enrollments was 2458% during those years, while campus-based enrollments grew at 66.9% in the same time frame. In the United States, from 2002 to 2012, ODE enrollments grew from over 1 million to over 5 million for a growth rate of over 300% during that decade. Even in Germany, in which ODE is a lower percentage of higher education enrollments, ODE enrollments grew from just over 69,000 in

2003 to over 154,000 in 2014 for a growth rate of 123% during that time frame. The overall effect has been that ODE enrollments have increased, in some countries dramatically, since the advent of online education.

Providers of ODE

The challenge of identifying student enrollments in ODE is partly due to the growth in the number institutions providing distance, particularly online, education. With the emerging digital media and technologies, the clear boundaries between conventional campus-based and distance teaching universities are blurring, and many higher education institutions are moving from single mode to dual mode activity. Historically, it used to be possible to identify which institutions offered online and distance education. As the lack of data in United Kingdom suggests, it has become more challenging to do so now that so many institutions are offering online education. There are now so many institutions offering ODE that it is difficult to know how many are doing so unless there are intentional efforts to gather this information.

The growth of ODE enrollments has been accompanied by three important trends about ODE providers: conventional ODE providers have increased their offerings; more campus-based institutions have become ODE providers; private institutions have grown in numbers and offerings.

Universities with a long history in open and distance education continue to provide ODE, often with increased offerings at institutions like Charles Sturt University in Australia, Athabasca University and TELUQ in Canada, Penn State University and University of Maryland University College in the United States, FernUniversität in Germany and the Open University in the United Kingdom. However, they are now often competing with institutions that historically did not offer ODE. In Australia, nearly 75% of all online enrollments are from six universities: Charles Sturt University, University of Southern Queensland, University of New England, Deakin University in Melbourne, Central Queensland University and the University of Tasmania. But most of the country's 49 universities also have some online enrollments. In Brazil, institutions have to be authorized by the federal government to provide ODE courses. There are 177 of the 2386 universities that are currently authorized to offer distance education at the university level. They offer a total of 3935 different courses. In Canada, over 80% of all ODE course enrollments are from institutions that are campus-based that also offer courses and programs that are fully online, or a mix of campus and online.

The ODE landscape is more competitive in each country than it ever has been. The growth of campus based DE offerings may be a threat to conventional ODE providers. Table 2 shows the growth in providers and competition in Germany.

Growth in German ODE enrollments is mainly from dual mode institutions—campus based institutions that offer blended or online courses. Indeed, the term dual mode university may be an outdated legacy of the twentieth century, as most campus - based universities in the U.S. and the U.K. also seem to be offering online courses and

Table 2 ODE enrollment growth in Germany

ODE growth rate	2005(%)	2007(%)	2009(%)	2011(%)	2012(%)	2013(%)	2014(%)
Dual mode institutions	26.1	4.8	26.0	3.2	57.2	15.6	23.2
Single mode	−7.7	12.5	39.7	34.7	−0.7	5.3	−5.1
Overall growth in DE	−2.6	11.0	37.2	29.3	7.2	7.3	0.9

programs. In the twenty-first century where digitization of education continues, it seems to be less important to distinguish between campus only and dual mode institutions.

ODE is increasingly provided by private universities—universities not receiving public funding from the government. There are two types of private universities, not-for-profit and for-profit. The Massachusetts Institute of Technology (MIT) in the United States is an example of a private not-for-profit university. Even their MOOC operation, EdX, is a nonprofit. Private sector campus-based for-profit universities have been operating for decades in Australia, the UK and the U.S. For-profit DE providers have also been in existence since the nineteenth century. However, it is with the advent of the Internet that for-profit universities have grown in number and offerings of ODE courses and programs. Among the most recognized examples of a for-profit institution is the University of Phoenix in the U.S. It is an ODE provider in the sense that it offers DE and has an open admissions policy, perhaps because it is a for-profit institution.

For-profit ODE is more common in some countries than others. For-profit ODE is minimal in Canada where there are almost no private, for-profit online universities, as Bates states in his chapter. In contrast in Brazil, it is the main source of ODE enrollments. Figure 1 shows how the overall growth of ODE enrollments has been almost parallel with the growth of ODE enrollments in private, especially for-profit, institutions.

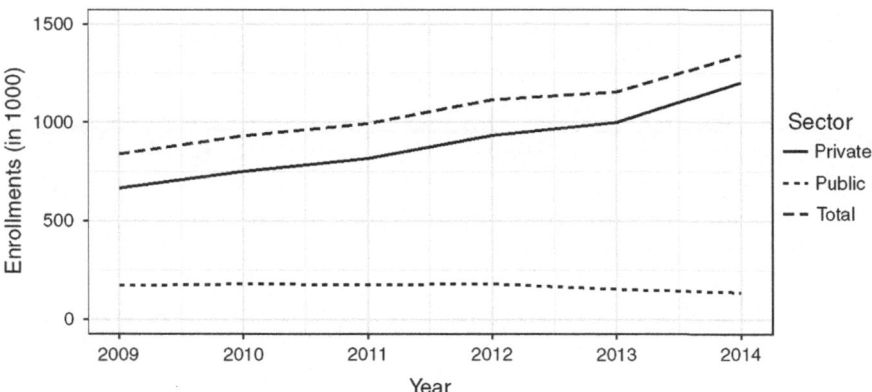

Fig. 1 Brazil ODE enrollments in public and private universities

A spectrum of the role of public to private institutions in providing ODE providers is illustrated in Fig. 2. The spectrum shows that ODE is dominated by public and private non-profit institutions in most countries covered in this volume.

However, in Brazil, and likely other countries, ODE is dominated by for-profit institutions. In 2009, 79.4% of ODE was delivered by private institutions in Brazil. By 2014, 89.6% of ODE was provided by for-profit institutions.

The Role of ICTs

An important part of the growth of ODE has been shape of ODE—the design and delivery of distance education using ICTs. It is notable that Germany has the lowest enrollments of students taking ODE courses among the six countries, as well as the lowest percentage of higher education students taking ODE. It is not surprising given that higher education is free in Germany, and there are now over 400 higher education institutions in this rather densely populated country. It also seems to be the country where more distance education courses are offered in correspondence and blended learning than in other countries. In Australia, Canada, the United States and the United Kingdom, ODE is now nearly synonymous with online education. In Brazil, online education has become what mobile phones have become in many countries, a leapfrog technology. Leap-frog technologies allow countries to leap over generations of technology that require infrastructure (e.g. landline phones), to a more recent ICT. This allows for superseding the old infrastructure requirements. Online education is a leapfrog technology for DE. Instead of investing in broadcast or videoconferencing systems infrastructure, countries can focus on cellular and broadband infrastructure. While there are cautions about leaving correspondence, radio and other forms of ODE—especially to provide access for people in underdeveloped regions—certainly the growth in ODE seems to be based on online education. With the development of online learning, ODE clearly moved into the mainstream of higher education systems.

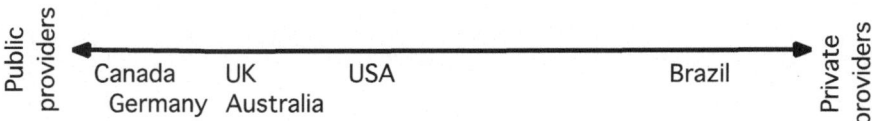

Fig. 2 Spectrum of public and private providers of ODE by country

The Role of Government

The changes in ODE occur in a context of government educational policies and regulations. In Australia, Brazil, and the United Kingdom the federal level of government controls higher education policy and regulation. Higher education in Canada and Germany is the responsibility of the province or state level of government. In the United States, public institutions are responsibility of the state, but public, private not-for-profit and private-for-profit institutions are affected by federal government regulations. The government context of ODE varies from high regulation countries to low regulation countries. Brazil is a high regulation country where all providers of ODE need to be authorized by the federal government. Government has to give permission for initiating ODE, and at times approving content and tuition costs. Governments have also helped foster ODE through educational policy initiatives to increase access, digitization, and ICT oriented education, like digital literacy initiatives. In Australia and Brazil, federal educational policies around digitization have helped accelerate the changes and growth of ODE. In Canada, these have occurred mainly at the provincial level, notably in Ontario and British Columbia. At the other end of ODE regulation is the United States. While U.S. educational policies vary from state to state, overall there it has been much more of a laissez-faire attitude about allowing institutions and businesses to make their own decisions about entering or expanding into distance education. However, state governments can set tuition fees. More recently, concerns about financial malfeasance of students in online education have led to post hoc regulations at the federal level about how student financial aid can be used by all online education providers.

The Function of ODE

The data on ODE enrollments and providers suggests that distance education is an increasingly important part of the higher education system in most countries. ODE seems to play three major functions in higher education systems: increasing access; providing flexibility; and abetting in the larger digital transformation of higher education. In some places, particularly Brazil, ODE continues to play an access mission that distance education has historically played. ODE is providing access to education for those who cannot get physical or, in some cases admissions, access to higher education. The immense growth in enrollments and providers suggests a large demand for higher education access that ODE is meeting faster than campus-based education. The access mission of ODE is likely still important in other countries particularly from institutions that have an open admissions policy, like the OU in the UK. In Germany, the Ministry of Education and Research is supporting higher education institutions with 250 million Euros in an "Open Education" funding program to develop a "lifelong learning" profile. Hundreds of new study programs have been developed by conventional campus-based universities in a blended learning format to provide flexible learning opportunities for non-traditional students.

Thus, ODE enrollments are partly growing from students who are already on campus and increasingly taking online courses. ODE is playing the role of providing flexible education options for conventional undergraduate, graduate, continuing education and adult students. The growth of distance education in Australia, Canada, Germany, the U.S. and the U.K. has been increasingly by institutions providing more options for students. In the United States, more than 80% of institutions with more than 1000 students offer some distance education courses (Allen and Seaman 2014, p. 14). In Europe, online education is not the domain of ODE institutions but now a common part of conventional higher education institutions" (Gaebel et al. 2014). In Canada, the growth of online learning has been substantially driven by on campus institutions.

Finally, ODE is, for many institutions, part of a larger phenomenon about the digitization of higher education. Latchem points out in his chapter on Australia that the growth of blended learning is blurring the distinction between on campus and distance education. Bates states that in Canada online education has moved many institutions towards increased blended learning as well as distance education. The growth of distance education, online education and blended learning is part of what Selwyn has called "the wider enmeshing of digital processes and practices within higher education" (Selwyn 2014). All functions within higher education are becoming digitized including communication, administration, research process and publications, and library services. The teaching functions, via full DE or blended, are just another manifestation of the digital transformation of universities.

Due to these functions, ODE has helped expand higher education as a whole. In Australia, Brazil and the United States ODE is more overtly an important part of the growth of higher education. In Australia, the increased use of digital technologies via distance and blended learning is an important part of the growth of postsecondary education. In the United States, university and college enrollments are mainly growing in online education. In Brazil, tertiary education is growing exponentially, mainly because of distance education.

Trends and Future Challenges

On a macro level, open and distance education is being affected by two major factors: the global growth in demand for education and the digital revolution. Notably, there seems to be less influence on ODE from globalization—the increasingly borderless economic and social exchanges. ODE still seems to function mainly, though not wholly, within a nation state. There is not much indication that non-domestic enrollments constitute a large percentage of ODE demand. There are two exceptions. In the United Kingdom, out-of-country for-credit enrollments in ODE may be as large as internal demand. Secondly, there is substantial out-of-country enrollments in many countries for non-credit ODE, such as MOOCs.

Practically, these two major factors, demand and digitization, manifest as important trends and challenges for ODE that are worth noting for students, teachers, designers, researchers, administrators and policy makers. First, ODE will likely continue to grow and to be an important part of meeting the expanding demand for higher education. This has led to many new entrants in ODE in Australia, Brazil, Canada, Germany, the United Kingdom and the United States. These include public and private for-profit institutions. For-profits exist to address a demand that public and private not-for-profit institutions may not be able to meet. In Canada and Germany, the demand for higher education may be met by public institutions offering ODE. In Brazil, the demand certainly has not been met.

Second, ODE is helping to foster more competition in the field of higher education. Education is unlike most other sectors of a society or economy. It has historically had a very strong collegial dynamic. Indeed, the word collegial has the same Latin origins as college. Both come from the word *collegium*, which means partnership or group in which each member has approximately equal power. Certainly, there has always been a competitive element to education at all levels. School and university rankings at local, national and international levels are at least partly a manifestation of competition. However problematic rankings may be, they continue to be part of the educational landscape and may inform educational choice decisions for many students. The growth of ODE expands the scale and geographical size of competition among institutions within and, to a lesser extent, outside of countries.

Third, growth of ODE is a conduit, among others, by which ICTs are potentially changing the higher education sector to becoming more of a private good.[1] Many public and private higher education institutions are charging students more for ODE programs, particularly for graduate programs. Education was and is often subsidized by the state and students paid only a portion of the cost of providing education. Historically, education in many countries is seen as a public good, suggesting that public investment and subsidizing in education is important because society as a whole, benefits from a more educated populace. The growth of ODEs is not just allowing for new entrants, approaches and services in higher education. It is changing how people think of the function and role of the education. Now, it is increasingly the case that students are being asked to pay the full costs of their education. Whether a good is public or private is ultimately about who pays for it. In Brazil, Canada and the United States at least, increasingly in many ODE programs students are paying for more of the cost of their education. The idea that education is a private good has been advocated by key institutions like the World Bank, that argue that private sector education is an important way to expand educational access and improve quality (Devarajan 2014). The growing acceptance of education as a private good was forecast in a sense already by Noble (2001) who argued that expanded online education would create digital diploma mills. ODE increases the growth of mass

---

[1]For economists, a good is public if it is non-exclusive and non-rivalrous. Non-exclusive means that I cannot exclude you from having it if I have the good. If I have street lighting, I cannot exclude you from consuming street lighting, without effort to block the lighting from you. Non-rivalrous means that you consuming it doesn't lessen my ability to consume it. If you are walking on a well light street, I can also benefit from that street. In this sense, formal education is often a private good.

higher education by making education a private good. Nowhere is this more evident than in Brazil.

Fourth, while there is increased competition in ODE, the barriers for new entrants in open and distance education are high. This has more to do with higher education generally than ODE specifically. Higher education is in a trust market (Winston 1997). An organization cannot be an educational start-up as a provider of higher education. This may not apply to training or micro-credit organizations. Trust is earned not in years but decades. It took the Open University of the UK decades to develop their good reputation. Education is not a product or service like most others. Existing institutions can have a decided advantage. They have a history and reputation. In Brazil, Litto points out that many for-profit new entrants, work around this barrier, by buying existing institutions and using their brand. They are partnering with, or acquire existing institutions and expanding their role into the ODE sector. They recognize that having a reputation, history and a future is important for providers of ODE.

Finally, ODE will likely continue to change shape as the digital transformation of higher education expands. This poses an existential challenge for conventional distance educators. As the popularity of ODE has grown in most countries on the demand and supply side, and digitization has created a convergence between on campus and online education, it has asked if distance education is ending. Likely ODE will continue to be important, if only because there are still students who will continue to be under-served by conventional education. However, distance educators cannot be complacent. They will need to address ongoing changes of new ICTs, the expanded competition of new entrants and increased demand for a quality educational experience in open and distance education.

The initial challenge for governments, researchers and institutional providers of ODE is to create and apply frameworks for analyzing a sector that is dramatically changing. Such frameworks would need to account for: the changing student demand, demographics and needs; the mission, goals and regulations of educational providers; the type and number of new entrants; and the creation of alternatives to conventional credentials, as educators, companies, and industry groups are offering new types of credentials. Ultimately the goal of such a framework should be to allow governments and institutions to develop not just internal management plans but also more competitive strategies. Such strategies will need to account for the mission of the institution, including their perspective of education as a public or private good. The creation of analytical frameworks is necessary because, as the chapters in this book illustrate in detail, ODE will continue to change in shape, size and location in Australia, Europe and the Americas. One such a framework is provided in the next volume in this series, on ODE in Asia, Africa and the Middle East.

References

Allen, I. E., & Seaman. J. (2014). *Grade change: Tracking online education in the United States*. Babson Survey Research Group and Quahog Research Group.

Devarajan, S. (2014). *Education as if economics mattered*. http://blogs.worldbank.org/futuredevelopment/education-if-economics-mattered.

Gaebel, M., Kupriyancva, V., Morais, R., & Colucci, E. (2014). *E-learning in European higher education institutions*. Belgium: European University Association.

HESA. (2016). Introduction—Students 2015/16. https://www.hesa.ac.uk/data-and-analysis/publications/students-2015-16/introduction.

Noble, D. F. (2001). *Digital diploma mills: The automation of higher education*. New York: Monthly Review Press.

Seaman, J., Allen, I.E. & Seaman, J. (2018). *Grade Increase: Tracking Distance Education in the United States*. Babson Survey Research Group and Quahog Research Group.

Selwyn, N. (2014). *Digital technology and the contemporary university: Degrees of digitization*. London: Routledge.

Winston, G. C. (1997). Why can't a college be more like a firm? *Change: The Magazine for Higher Learning 29*(5), 33–38.